I NEVER KNEW YOU

FROM TRAGEDY TO TRIUMPH

Arise to your purpose,
Iris Wainright

IRIS WAINRIGHT

Trilogy Christian Publishers
A Wholly Owned Subsidiary of Trinity Broadcasting Network
2442 Michelle Drive
Tustin, CA 92780

For information, address Trilogy Christian Publishing
Rights Department, 2442 Michelle Drive, Tustin, Ca 92780.
Trilogy Christian Publishing/ TBN and colophon are trademarks
of Trinity Broadcasting Network.
For information about special discounts for bulk purchases,
please contact Trilogy Christian Publishing.
Manufactured in the United States of America

10 9 8 7 6 5 4 3 2 1
Library of Congress Cataloging-in-Publication Data is available.
ISBN 978-1-63769-980-5
ISBN 978-1-63769-981-2 (ebook)

DEDICATION

I dedicate this book, first and foremost, to God, whose grace, forgiveness, and unconditional love have brought me through life's challenges. I praise You for your guidance and wisdom in telling my story. God, You have been faithful, and Your promises are true.

"And we know (with great confidence) that God (who is deeply concerned about us) causes all things to work together (as a plan) for good for those who love God, to those who are called according to His plan and purpose" (Romans 8:28, AMP).

Chris, you are the love of my life. I want to thank you for being the husband I have always desired. Your kindness, forgiveness, and unconditional love over the years have given me strength and confidence to be transparent in writing this book.

I love you more than yesterday but less than tomorrow.

And to Laurie, Derek, Delaney, Daughtry, Angela, Mark, Caleb, Ryan, Micah, Bailey, Scout, Layton, and Basil, I am proud that you call me Mom and Mimi. Thank you for being God's greatest gifts to me.

I love you to the moon and back and forward.

ACKNOWLEDGMENTS

Mark and Olene Arnett, thank you for allowing me to share some of your scars in your life with others. Mark, you will always be my *little brother*. Move forward in God's plan for your life and finish strong in the Lord. I love you both.

Pastor William (Bill) and Dorothy Jean Ligon, Dr. Bill Gothard, and Pastor Dale and Donna Blair, thank you for being faithful to your calling. You have all taught God's Word with compassion and clarity. I will be forever grateful for your wisdom and influence in my life. You have been an example of faithfulness in serving the Lord for years. Thank you for your unconditional love.

Charles Durham, Billy Godwin, Helen Ledford, and Pat Ulmer have been faithful friends over the years. A special appreciation to my friend forever, Pat Ulmer, who also assisted in editing and so much more.

I love and appreciate each of you.

ENDORSEMENTS

I *had no idea how God was going to impact my life by reading Iris Wainright's book, "I Never Knew You: From Tragedy to Triumph." You will understand this by the following endorsement. Very few books have a major impact on my life. Iris' gripping life testimony is such a book. I began reading it at 2 a.m., and at 6 a.m., I reluctantly put it down to get some sleep. A few hours later, I got up and finished her book.*

Seventy years ago, I dedicated my life to working with teenagers. After reading this book, I realized that I must write a book on how to prepare children for the tragedies of life.

You cannot read Iris' life story without asking the question, "Why did God let all this happen to her?" There is an important answer. We are not a body with a soul and spirit; we are a spirit in a body that also has a soul. The real "you" is your spirit! When God allows something to happen to our body, He compensates by making us "Mighty in Spirit," as in the case of Daniel, whose body was damaged by making him a eunuch, which means that he would never have children; but he became Mighty in Spirit.

The evidence of Iris being "Mighty in Spirit" was her ability to know in her spirit that her mother was dying in a motel. Also, in her ability to experience genuine salvation and forgiveness. We are saved by the power of God's grace through our faith.

Jesus identifies three levels of faith that correspond to our three brains. "No faith" is a response to our head brain. It is simply an intellectual exercise, which can easily change. "You believe that God is one; you do well, even the demons believe, and shudder" (James 2:19, ESV). Our heart's brain has "little faith." It is good but shallow with "no root" (Luke 8:13, ASV). "Great faith" is in our reins (gut-brain) (Revelations 2:23, KJV). It is a faith for which we will die. When we are ready to die for Jesus, we are ready to receive Him as our personal Savior. We confirm this intent by a symbolic death experience in baptism.

This is extremely important because many people make a confession of faith with their head-brain, and nothing happens. Because of all that Iris endured, she had great faith and a Mighty Spirit through Christ, her Savior. It was Iris' book that inspired me to write my book: "A Preteen Guide to Conquer Every Trial!"

I rejoice in the powerful results of reading Iris' book!

—Dr. Bill Gothard
International Speaker
President of Embassy University
Founder of the Basic Youth Conflicts Seminar
Author of *A Preteen Guide to Conquer Every Trial!*

It is with great honor that I endorse my dear friend Iris Wainright's book, "I Never Knew You: From Tragedy to Triumph."

There is a technique that the Japanese use to repair broken pottery called Kintsugi, the Art of Repair. This is where they take the broken pieces of pottery and put them back together with lacquer dusted with gold, silver, or platinum, making the piece of pottery much more valuable.

Just like Jesus Christ did for Iris' life, He took the broken and shattered pieces of her life, a total mess, and filled it with His own precious blood, something much more precious and more valuable than gold, silver, or platinum. Jesus' blood binds the broken pieces of our lives together, creating a beautiful story to be shared like Iris has in this book, not out of a place of brokenness but out of a place of complete wholeness.

This is a must-read for anyone who has been abused mentally, physically, or sexually. You will find that it is not your past that defines you; it is who you are in Christ. You are a son & daughter of the Most High God, a beautiful life that He can repair if you only reach out to Him.

—**Donna Grisham**
Guest Relations, Production Coordinator, *Sid Roth's It's Supernatural* Host of *The Real Prochoice Show, ISN Network*
Author of *Journeys of Choice: There is Hope in The Midst of an Unplanned Pregnancy*

I have known Chris and Iris Wainright for over twenty years. I was their pastor at Cornerstone Church when they moved to Greenville, South Carolina, in 1990. I had no idea of the past abuse and pain Iris faced throughout her life. I have only witnessed her love and spiritual maturity for her Savior, Jesus Christ. It was her relationship with her heavenly Father that empowered her to forgive the abuse of her earthly father and mother.

It takes great courage for Iris to reveal her abusive past to everyone else. She knows her identity is not defined by her past but only by the life and power of a loving God to heal and set someone free.

I encourage anyone who has dealt with abuse to read "I Never Knew You: From Tragedy to Triumph." You will experience the hope and freedom that can only be found in Jesus Christ.

—**Pastor Dale Blair**
Retired Pastor of Cornerstone Church
Greenville, South Carolina 29615

TABLE OF CONTENTS

FOREWORD 15

PREFACE 17

INTRODUCTION 21

PART 1: IDA'S STORY 23

CHAPTER 1: GERMANY 1923............................25

CHAPTER 2: NO WAY OF ESCAPE............................29

CHAPTER 3: UP CLOSE & PERSONAL............................41

CHAPTER 4: AN OFFICER & A GENTLEMAN?............................47

CHAPTER 5: LAND OF PROMISE............................57

PART 2: IRIS' STORY 63

CHAPTER 1: GRIT OR GRITS............................65

CHAPTER 2: DEAD MAN WALKING............................71

CHAPTER 3: SHAME HAS A VOICE............................75

CHAPTER 4: THE HIDING PLACE............................81

CHAPTER 5: CALIFORNIA OR BUST............................85

CHAPTER 6: CHILDREN SHOULD BE SEEN, NOT HEARD...89

CHAPTER 7: LITTLE BLACK BOOK............................93

CHAPTER 8: SLEEPING WITH STRANGERS............................101

CHAPTER 9: MY BROTHER'S KEEPER............................107

CHAPTER 10: I SCREAM FOR ICE CREAM!.................111

CHAPTER 11: "ICH LIEBE DICH"...........................115

CHAPTER 12: AMERICAN PRINCESS......................121

CHAPTER 13: WHAT IS YOUR EMERGENCY?.................127

CHAPTER 14: GOOD TIMES ARE HERE....................135

CHAPTER 15: MOMMIE DEAREST..........................139

CHAPTER 16: FOOL'S HILL...............................143

CHAPTER 17: TON OF BRICKS...........................151

CHAPTER 18: CRUISE OF A LIFETIME....................157

PART 3: THE REST OF THE STORY 175

CHAPTER 1: EVERYBODY LOVES LOVE!......................177

CHAPTER 2: ANCHORS AWAY...............................183

CHAPTER 3: IT FEELS LIKE HOME.........................189

CHAPTER 4: CYCLE OF ABUSE............................197

CHAPTER 5: ONLY GOD!.................................203

CHAPTER 6: JUST AS I AM...............................207

CHAPTER 7: BUMMER LAMB...............................211

CHAPTER 8: PITIFUL OR POWERFUL......................217

CHAPTER 9: I AM WHO YOU SAY I AM..................227

CHAPTER 10: I HEAR ANGEL WINGS......................237

CHAPTER 11: ALL BETS OFF.............................245

CHAPTER 12: I GOT THIS!..............................249

CHAPTER 13: I NEVER KNEW YOU.........................255

EPILOGUE   267

A FINAL WORD   269

PROCLAIMED BLESSING   271

A FATHER SPEAKS A PROCLAIMED BLESSING OVER IRIS.....271
A FATHER SPEAKS A PROCLAIMED BLESSING OVER CHRIS..275

AUTHORS PICTURES   277

REFERENCES & HELP   283

BIBLE SCRIPTURES   285

ABOUT THE AUTHOR   289

FOREWORD

*M*any emotionally, physically, and sexually wounded people will find the road to healing and new life after reading Iris Wainright's book "I Never Knew You: From Tragedy to Triumph." Her freedom to share the details of her past tragedies from her childhood, especially abuse from her father and mother, has resulted in this book which will be popularized through the years to bring many people from their tragedy to triumph and into personal, saving relationships with Jesus Christ.

I was privileged to know Chris and Iris Wainright as their pastor at Christian Renewal Church in Brunswick, Georgia, before they moved to Greenville, South Carolina. I have known them for over forty years.

It was obvious during those years that Iris had a strong, growing relationship with the Lord Jesus Christ and that her baptism in the Holy Spirit gave her spiritual power to be a witness to many people. A highlight of her Christian journey was when she received grace to forgive her father and mother, both of whom had seriously abused her in her childhood.

Iris quickly learned the power of the spoken blessing, which broke verbal curses spoken over her by her parents. She is mighty in Spirit and has spoken many blessings over her husband, daughters, grandchildren, and other members of her family. They, too, have experienced the presence and salvation of the Lord for themselves. Iris has beautifully embraced the biblical principles of faith, love, and forgiveness, overcoming the many challenges of abuse.

Reading Iris' book is so very important for every person who seeks healing from abuse. You can discover the loving presence and power of the Lord Jesus Christ in your own lives.

I am honored to endorse Iris' book, which will challenge, inspire, and encourage any reader.

—William (Bill) T. Ligon, Sr.
Founder of Christian Renewal Church
Founder of Fellowship Christian Churches and Ministers
Missionary, International Speaker
Author of *Discipleship: The Jesus View, Imparting the Blessing and Successful Steps to Maturity.*

PREFACE

Writing *I Never Knew You: From Tragedy to Triumph* has been a long journey. As you will read in my book, Chris, my husband, did not know about my past until after I wrote this book. He was resting in his recliner, watching television, when I interrupted his news program. I quickly said, "Honey, I have a lot to do today, so I will be home late. While I am gone, would you please read this manuscript I have written? It's still not finished." Without looking up, he answered, "Of course, what is it about?"

"It's about my mother and my life. I want to be honest with you before I am honest with anyone else." I quickly left the house before he could question me any further. I was gone for hours, afraid of what Chris would say when I returned. I was extremely nervous as I returned home and made my way through the kitchen to the den, where he was still seated in his recliner, with my manuscript in his hand. He looked up with tears in his eyes. He held up the manuscript and said, "I could not put your manuscript down. Why have you not told me about your past?" He was not ashamed, nor did I feel his rejection that I had feared all my married life.

My best friend, Judy Durham, approached me after I spoke at a luncheon and said, "Iris, I noticed the people's reaction to your message. No one can believe what you have lived through. People came up to me asking for your book. I do believe you should write a book on your life. It would help people understand what God will do in overcoming the traumatic events in their own lives and give them hope. God has truly been with you." The Holy Spirit had already prompted me to start sharing my testimony by publishing a book. When Judy and I met to discuss writing my book, I handed her a notebook. She replied, "Thank you, but what is this for?"

"For you to write my book. Just ask me questions, and I will tell you about my past."

She smiled, "Iris, I am not writing your story; you are. You lived it, not me."

Startled, I nervously said, "You have helped so many authors in writing their book. Besides all the books you have written. You are the writer. I cannot do this. I thought you would write this book about my life."

Judy laughed and confidently said, "I am a *writing coach*. I will help you along the way to stay on track writing your book. I will review, edit, and keep you focused. The Holy Spirit will guide you on what to remember and what to write."

That day I began my journey. I wanted to give up many times, but Judy would only allow me time to heal from the pain of my memories while encouraging me to finish my book. You are an amazing friend.

I could not have finished this book without your coaching.

INTRODUCTION
I Never Knew You

Who in the world do you think you are to second-guess God? Do you for one moment suppose any of us knows enough to call God into question? Clay does not talk back to the fingers that mold it, saying, why did you shape me like this? Isn't it obvious that a potter has a perfect right to shape one lump of clay into a vase for holding flowers and another into a pot for cooking beans?

Romans 9:20 (MSG)

For years I did not want anyone to know me because they would surely cast me aside like the broken vessel that I was. I believed I had to keep my shocking series of events hidden in the dark places where hopefully no one would discover the real me. I refused to allow God to mold my life like a lump of clay into a vessel that He created to serve others. I chose to be the vessel I wanted others to see, hoping that vessel would be pleasing to everyone. It became an impossible task.

Doom to you! You pretend to have the inside track. You shut God out and work behind the scenes, plotting the future as if you knew everything, acting mysterious, never showing your hand. You have everything backward! You treat the potter as a lump of clay. Does a book say to its author, "He didn't write a word of me?" Does a meal say to the woman who cooked it, "She had nothing to do with this?"

Isaiah 29:15-16 (MSG)

Everyone has a testimony to tell, and this is my testimony, inspired by true events. Some names have been changed to respect their privacy. This story begins with my mother's life during the devastation of World War II. There is a lot of sorrow and agony in "tragedy" but an abundance of "joy" and "peace" in the triumph. Circumstances and tragedies will try to rewrite this love story. But the potter knows how to form the clay so that in the end, after going through the fire, we have become a chosen vessel.

PART 1: IDA'S STORY

IF YOU'RE WALKING THROUGH HELL, WALK FASTER

Night brought terror to Karlsruhe, Germany, as sirens screamed their piercing warning to seek shelter. Bombs dropped out of the sky with a terrifying whistling sound that stopped but for a moment before the deadly explosion that destroyed whole buildings in an instant.

Families left their shelters as the all-clear sirens announced it was temporarily safe to come out. Ida felt great relief that she had escaped death, only to then face the horror of the loss of family, friends, and neighbors. Living could be worse than death. Her heart beat with fear for what she would find; loved ones lost, homes destroyed and left burning, destruction beyond comprehension...

My name is Ida Klara Lina Zubiller. In Germany, my name is pronounced "Eee-da." I am an only child of Sophie Bertha Lampart Zubiller. I am also the mother of Iris Wainright, who is the author of this book. I think it is important for you to first know me and understand the beginning of my life in Germany. It had a great impact on me and a greater impact on the life of Iris, my only daughter. Let us begin with *my story*.

CHAPTER 1
GERMANY, 1923

The ominous dark clouds of the afternoon rolled across the German sky, shedding their raindrops like tears, seeming to join with my cries as I came into the world. My mama's heartbroken tears flowed as she returned to the painful memory of my papa, who had abandoned her. Mama was fearful. Her thoughts were troubled. *What am I going to do? I am only twenty-two years old, and I will have no family because of this baby. My parents' social standing with their aristocratic attitude will not allow the presence of an unwed mother and her bastard child. What is to become of my baby and me without a family or husband to take care of us?*

The sound of the rain hitting the window increased, as did her resolve to survive. My mother's name was Sophie. As she gave birth to her daughter, her courage began to assert itself deeply within her German soul. I came into this world just as cataclysmic changes were occurring in the world, all around me. It was August 13, 1923, and the birthplace was Karlsruhe, Germany. I did not know any of the story of my birth until years later. I was seven years old when I began questioning in my mind why most of my friends had Papas, but I did not.

One early Saturday morning, I sat at the kitchen table as Mama stood with her back to me, cooking a pan of eggs and potatoes. She bent down to take bread out of the oven. She cut a few slices and slathered them with butter and a generous serving of her homemade strawberry jam. My mouth watered. The smell of strong coffee wafted through the kitchen. Without thinking, I blurted out, "Mama, why do I not have a papa like Hilda and Brigitta?"

Mama slowly turned toward me with a surprised look on her face. She laid the plate down roughly on the table in front of me. Her eyes changed from surprise to anger as she said, "I knew this day would come." Her reaction frightened me. She stood very still and glared at me. Finally, she replied sternly, "Your papa, Johann Jacob, was not an honorable man. For years, I thought we were very much in love until the day I broke the news to him that I was expecting you. I thought he would be happy about our having a baby, but I soon discovered that a baby was unwelcome news to him. After I told him, he screamed at me, 'There is no room in my life for a wife and child.' He left the room and slammed the door. I never saw him again." I was too shocked at this news to respond. "Ida, you do not need a papa. We are fine without a man to take care of us," she answered in a bitter voice. "Now that you know, you must never tell anyone the truth about your father. We must hide our shameful secret. You must tell the same lie that I tell everyone. Your father is dead." Mama looked off in the distance.

"But why? Why do we have to lie?" I asked.

Turning away from me, she said, "You do as I say."

Mama's stiff back told me that she was not going to say any more. I was too young to understand, but I was too frightened to ask again. I knew I had to accept her demand. I did not ask any more questions as I began my life of lies.

Changes were occurring all around me.

— CHAPTER 2 —
NO WAY OF ESCAPE

*W*orld War I ended with a devastating loss to Germany. The middle-class standard of living for a German family that so many enjoyed was altered by events outside of Germany, beyond their control. The Great Depression of 1929 began casting Germany into poverty and deep misery. Everyone began looking for a solution, any solution. Many in Germany began to believe that Adolph Hitler was the solution. He would, overnight, be their savior. Following the death of President Hindenburg on August 2, 1934, Hitler united the chancellorship and presidency under the new title of Führer (meaning the absolute authority). The Nazi Party grew to be the largest elected party in Germany. Hitler's first six years in power resulted in rapid economic recovery from the Great Depression, which gave him significant popular support[1].

The sunset had been particularly spectacular this evening. The beautiful purple and orange hues seemed to send a message of peacefulness and calm. It was September 1, 1939. Mama sat on the couch in our living room as I sat on the floor fiddling

---

1   www.wikipedia.org

with the radio dial, searching for a radio station with an update of the latest world events. The efforts and successes of Hitler and the Nazi Party were broadcast every evening, filling us with great optimism that our way of life would soon be restored to us. Finally, I found the broadcast I was searching for as the announcer began, "And now, a word from our glorious Führer." Hitler came on the radio and proclaimed, "Today is a glorious day for Germany! Our troops have successfully entered Poland from the west." Hitler then spoke sternly to the Polish people, "From now on, a bomb will be met with a bomb."

We could hear on the radio the enthusiastic roar of the crowds. Mama and I looked at each other as tears filled our eyes. I sat very still and pondered what this would mean for us. I was only sixteen years old when France and Britain declared war on Germany, starting World War II. Then on September 17, 1939, Soviet troops invaded Poland from the east.

As the years passed, life became more difficult, despite Hitler's promises of prosperity. We hoarded what we could find so we had something we could sell or use to barter. Life was unbearably hard for Mama and me, especially without a man to provide for and protect us.

Hitler wanted Germany's youth to be indifferent to pain, *showing no weakness or tenderness.* All the young boys that were twelve years old or older were taken to serve in the "Hitler Youth." They learned how to be soldiers and worked on farms since all the farmers had gone to war.

Whenever I looked in the mirror at my blond hair and blue eyes, blessed with a strong will to survive, I realized I qualified to be the Führer's ideal Aryan German citizen. From the outside, I looked like a loyal citizen, but on the inside, I recoiled at the cruelty of Hitler's regime.

Food was rationed with food stamps that were color-coded. Blue stamps were for meat, white for sugar, green for eggs, and purple was fruit. Mama could no longer enjoy her cup of coffee in the morning. Coffee was nowhere to be found. Medicine was being used for the soldiers. Toilet paper was a luxury. We accepted that life as we knew it was now over.

During this time, Mama met and married a tall, much younger man named Hans Minet. He was handsome, even though he often wore a black patch over his left eye to hide a war injury that had left an indentation beside his eye. He had lost his sight in one of his eyes while fighting as a young German soldier in the war. Despite his injury, he was still able to serve as a soldier in the new German army.

Mama was excited whenever Hans got a short leave and returned home. But after his leave was over, Hans had to board the train with other soldiers from the city returning to his duty station. Hans would hang out from the train window waving and yelling, *Ich Liebe dich,* Sophia" (which translates "I love you, Sophia"). Mama cried back, *"Ich Liebe dich liebling"* (I love you, darling), as she ran alongside the train until she could no longer keep up, then returned to me on the platform.

Sirens went off day and night to warn people of danger. There were different sirens that meant different things—one meant to take cover before the raid started; another siren was to announce that it was safe to leave the air raid shelters. The bombs made a whistling sound as they dropped and an ear-splitting noise when they hit the ground.

Most of the bombing campaigns against Germany were conducted by the British at night. Blackouts were ordered, and it was my responsibility to carefully cover our windows at night with our dark blackout curtains. This kept the light inside our home so the enemy aircraft could not navigate to their targets in civilian areas.

At night I trembled with fear as I carefully peeked from behind the dark blackout curtains, watching the sky light up from the deadly bombers dropping their bombs over my beloved city. The constant fear of death was all around me, and my nerves kept me sick to my stomach. I could not sleep except from extreme exhaustion.

Daylight brought the screams of neighbors lying in the streets burning to death. Even in the daytime, bombers came. If I was not home, I would hear Mama frantically yelling "Eda" as she ran through the streets of Karlsruhe, trying to find me to take me to a bunker. After she found me, we would run to the nearest bunker for safety, where we would stay for hours or even days at a time, often with little or no food or water. The sounds of people crying and begging for food in the shelter threatened to drive us insane.

I recall that winter was one of the harshest and most unforgiving winter seasons. Christmas, usually filled with joy and celebration, quickly approached; but so many people were filled with sadness. At night the streetlamps were off because of the blackout. It was dangerous to walk the town alone in the pitch black.

One holiday evening, I was hurrying through the streets of Karlsruhe, trying to get home from my best friend Hilda's house. We exchanged simple gifts and fruit, laughed, and played, and sang traditional German Christmas songs such as "O Tannenbaum" (Oh, Christmas Tree).

I had missed the city's-imposed curfew. As I rounded the last corner towards my home, I was startled by a soldier who suddenly stepped out from the dark.

He did not speak as I tried to catch my breath. Shivering from the cold, I said, "Oh, you startled me. Good evening. I'm on my way home from my friend's house," I muttered.

I saw his eyes roaming up and down my slender young body. I realized that the soldier was not listening to anything I was saying. He suddenly grabbed my wrist and pulled me towards the cold dark alley.

"Take off your coat!" he commanded. Trembling, I obeyed him, dropping my coat in the filthy alley. The soldier tore open my blouse, exposing my young breast. He threw me to the ground as he hastily unzipped his pants. I laid dazed and filled with terror, too afraid to scream, knowing no one would come to my rescue for fear of their own life. Too often in the past, I had heard screams in the night. *Could the screams have come from other girls, faced with the same act of violence I was now facing?* I was all alone. I knew no help would be coming. I had no way of escape.

He quickly reached down and tore my undergarments away as he pressed his body on top of mine. I could smell the alcohol on his breath. The soldier was breathing heavily as he put his mouth on mine, but I fought his advances. I cried and begged, "Please, no, no!" but he ignored my pleas which only seemed to add to his excitement of having complete power over me.

"Shut up, or I will kill you!" he snarled.

I thought, *I must stay quiet, so he will let me live.* Then suddenly, he penetrated my body with such force I screamed out in agony. He quickly finished. He then got off me, stood up, zipped his pants, and fled, leaving me lying and bleeding in the dark, filthy alley. His stench lingered as I lay in shock, listening to the sounds around me. I heard his boots hitting the pavement as he ran off, like the rats that ran past my feet.

Shivering from the cold and shock, I stood up, crying. I picked up my ruined panties, pulled my torn blouse together, and took a deep breath. In excruciating pain, I slid my arms into my coat and wiped my mouth as if I could wipe the filth away. I felt dirty, ashamed, and disgusted. If only I could just crawl out of my skin.

In a daze, I looked up at the scorched building facade above me. It had been cut up unevenly by bombs. I thought to myself, *I'm like this damaged building. My body and soul are scarred from an act of violence, too. I have survived the violence, and I am still standing.*

Like the bomb, the soldier's horrific act only took a moment of time, but his act would last a lifetime in my soul. Putting one foot in front of the other, I slowly walked toward home as I determined no one could know. I had to get to my bedroom without my mother seeing me.

Many weeks later, the guilt, fear, and despicable shame from being violently sexually assaulted continued to torment me. The morning sickness only confirmed what I already suspected. I was pregnant! I was anguished with the thought of being a mother—something I did not desire, especially with his child.

Each night before I went to bed, I thought, *I could not do this alone, carrying the weight of this secret lie.* I did not have the courage to share with anyone what normally would have been happy news. I decided to try to find solace by going to the nearby Catholic church. As I entered the church, the soft light from the prayer candles at the altar gave me a sense of peace. People were kneeling, softly crying, while others loudly wailed in agony for God to deliver them from the horrors of war and the heartache of the death of their loved ones.

The bishop in the church noticed me as I sat in a pew, softly weeping. He approached me, saying, "You are safe in this sanctuary, my child." I received great comfort that night from the kind and welcoming words Father Friedrich spoke to me. As I began visiting more often, Father Friedrich would encourage me to confess my sins to him.

One night, armed with courage, I began opening my heart, whispering to the priest about the soldier raping me. I told in detail about the horrifying night that the soldier forced me into the dark alley. I also confessed to him that I was hiding the fact that I was pregnant. "You do not need to be afraid. God is with you," he promised.

I finally had someone I could trust, and I did not have to live with the pain of the memory from the assault alone. Father Friedrich became a father figure whom I could confide in and find the compassion I desperately needed. I often went to the church to receive his kindness. I looked forward to my visits with him. He always met me with a warm embrace, assuring me in his soothing voice, "Your secret is safe with me, my child."

This night was like any other night as I entered the church. After everyone had left the chapel, I found myself alone with Father Friedrich. "Take off your coat. It is warm in here." He came toward me, pulling out his hands which were scuttled into the folds of his cassock. He was speaking softly to me about his concern for me. Something did not feel right, so without saying a word, I turned to walk away. Suddenly I felt his large hands grab my shoulders while tightening his grip. Terror gripped my heart. I could not breathe.

This is not right, I thought, as I quickly glanced around to look for a way of escape. I looked back at Father Friedrich. I caught the look in his eyes, the same look I had seen in the soldier's eyes. He had only one thing on his mind, and he was not going to be denied. His hand reached out and stroked my long blond hair. The fear paralyzed me as I realized what was about to happen. I kept standing, frozen in time, unable to move, even though I knew his intent. He then calmly unbuttoned my shirt and began caressing my breast. Tears streamed down my face as he pulled me close to him. The roughness of his woolen cassock rubbed against my mature exposed breast. Once again, I begged, "Please, stop, stop, I want to go home." Struggling and pleading with him to stop did not discourage the bishop from forcing me to the floor of the chapel and raping me.

After Father Friedrich finished ravishing me, he rolled off me and stood up. He pulled up his pants, smoothed his cassock, and replaced his purple zucchetto skullcap. As he was leaving the sanctuary, he looked back at me, still lying on the floor. I felt so violated. He arrogantly said, "Ida, do not think you can tell anyone about tonight because no one will believe a pregnant tramp over a respected bishop." Father Friedrich had broken his vow of celibacy and the trust that I had so innocently placed in him.

I laid on the floor, curled up in a fetal position, still shaking, feeling dirty and disgusted from the ordeal, in a state of disbelief and shock. He was supposed to be my trusted friend and priest. He had promised to protect me and my private shameful dark secrets. After all, he was a man of God! A man who listened and offered forgiveness for their sins. It was like a nightmare that would not end. I sobbed uncontrollably.

I also knew that no one would ever believe that a Catholic bishop would violate a pregnant teenage girl. I would be blamed even though I was the victim of the crime. I thought to myself, *How many other young girls have also been seduced by this evil bishop's so-called care and compassion? How many has he lured into his devious, carnal secret life?* I felt sick to my stomach as I gathered my clothes and dressed. *How could this place of sanctuary and safety be a holy place of God? How can such evil exist in a holy place of God?* I slowly walked in a daze to my home. I began to say out loud, "I will survive."

My nights became filled with nightmares and flashbacks. When I closed my eyes trying to find sleep, the bishop's face leered down at me with a crazed, wild expression on his face. I could still feel the pressure of his large hands as he held me down, nearly suffocating me with the weight of his body. I could feel my body writhing under him, trying to escape, my head lashing from side to side as I pleaded, "No, no." I would break out of the dream, sweating, trembling, wailing, rocking back and forth, desperately longing for comfort and peace that I could not find. I felt I was going crazy, asking myself continuously, *What did I do to cause this to happen to me again?* It was the darkest, loneliest feeling I'd ever encountered. I could no longer go back to a place where there was no refuge. My youth was stolen from me.

The church became a place of betrayal.

CHAPTER 3
UP CLOSE AND PERSONAL

As the long days and even longer nights passed, I tried to hide my pregnancy. I didn't even tell my best friend, Hilda. I had lost my innocence and was forced to face adult decisions concerning my life and the life of my unborn baby. My disgrace caused me to isolate myself from the close relationship I always had with Mama. I could not bear the thought of her rejection. I had to keep my shocking incident secret from everyone.

As I walked past people on the street, I became convinced that they knew of my shame. Any whispers made me feel they knew and were talking about me. I was consumed with guilt and so ashamed as if it was my fault that I had been violently sexually assaulted twice. I thought maybe if I had not been out after curfew, it would not have happened. If only I had not gone to the chapel and told the bishop about the soldier raping me, he might not have lured me into another rape.

Time passed, and my disgrace was beginning to show. One afternoon, I walked to Hilda's home. When she answered the door, I burst into tears. "What's wrong?" she asked, holding out her arms to embrace me.

Falling into her arms, I whispered in her ear, "I have something to tell you."

"Come on in. No one is at home." I walked into her home and looked around nervously to be certain no one was home.

Then I began to tell Hilda, "I was raped!"

"No! What happened?"

"Remember, the night we opened gifts at your house, and I left late, after curfew? On the way home, I was startled and forced into an alley by a soldier, and he raped me. And now, I'm pregnant. I do not know what I am going to do."

"Have you told your mama?"

"I cannot. I'm too ashamed."

"You did not do anything wrong; what are you ashamed about?"

"I have not told you the whole story. I had been visiting the chapel on the corner for a couple of months, talking to Father Friedrich about that terrible night that the soldier raped me. I told him that I was pregnant. I thought he was being kind and understanding with his loving embraces every time I visited. One night when we were alone, he violently raped me too!"

Hilda gasped and grabbed me. "No, this is unbelievable! Oh my God, that is terrible! Ida, do not worry; somehow, we will get through this together. We must tell someone! You must tell your mama!"

Sobbing, I said, "I should have told Mama about what happened in that dark alley, but I was too scared. After Father Friedrich raped me too, I knew no one would believe me. I cannot tell her now; I just cannot."

"Now I understand why you've been so distant. You have changed, Ida. You are no longer fun to be around, and you have been so quiet and always upset. I thought I had done something to make you angry at me."

"I'm sorry. I should have told you earlier, but I do not know who to trust anymore with such awful secrets. I was afraid of how you would feel towards me."

"I will always be your friend. I do not know what we're going to do, but now that I know what you have been through, your secrets are safe with me. We will find a way together. Tell your mama you want to stay with me for a while. Don't worry, Ida; I helped Mama deliver my brother and sister. When the time comes, I can help you too."

"Yes, of course, I will find a way to come and live with you. Hilda, Mama likes you; she will let me stay with you. Thank you, thank you." Finally, I had someone who would help me. I was not going through this alone.

One bitterly cold winter morning, while Hilda's parents were away, I gave birth to a son in their damp, dark cellar. The warmth of the wood-burning stove staved off the cold. I laid holding my baby while love filled my heart, replacing the emptiness, disgust, and regret I had been feeling. He was so tiny and frail. After a couple of days, my baby son grew ill. I could not stop his crying, and I could feel him getting hotter and hotter. There was nothing I could do as I watched in horror as his breathing became more labored. Suddenly he stopped breathing.

The pain of delivering my son was nothing like the pain of him dying in my arms. I sobbed uncontrollably as my tears fell on my son's tiny dead face. I felt unbearable grief as I stared at the lifeless body of my baby. Hilda tried to take him from me, but I held him close as I stood in shock. "Ida, we will have to do something with his body. No one can know." There was only one thing to do. In shock, I gently wrapped my dead son in a small, thin, and wrinkled blanket, cuddled him for the last time. I placed him into the wood-burning stove. Hilda stood quietly, crying by my side. There were no words to comfort me as I collapsed to the floor, groaning and wailing in grief; the evidence of the birth of my son burned before our anguished tearful eyes. I thought that my shame would be burned away with my baby's body, but I was wrong.

As the days passed, I was tormented in my thoughts, constantly blaming myself for the death of my baby. I wondered, *Will I ever get over the death of my son? Do I have the right to ever be happy again?*

Hilda insisted, "We need to protect ourselves from men. We'll wear men's clothes and cut our hair short." From that day, whenever we went out, we wore men's clothes. Our disguise was working, but I could not hide my guilt. I was determined that no man would ever abuse me or have control over me again. I became bitter and suspicious of everyone I met, fearing that I could meet the same fate as I had already experienced.

As the war went on, it became clear that Jews were increasingly disappearing, and it was rumored that they were being killed. Mama and I tried to help the Jewish family that lived across the street. We shared our food and offered them a place to hide when the Nazi soldiers were in Karlsruhe. We knew the Nazi ideology. We were Gentile and were not allowed to associate or help Jewish neighbors.

One morning, Mama stared at me across from our kitchen table, then she said, "Ida, you know, if we get caught helping these Jews, we can be arrested and killed."

I angrily replied, "These are my friends. They are worth the risk. I cannot act like the Nazis with their prejudice and hatred. I will not be a monster. I refuse to follow their orders. I will not!" Mama was touched by my compassion and finally agreed. Each day, Mama and I faced new obstacles to our survival. We witnessed and experienced the many horrors of the Nazi regime up close and personal.

After Adolf Hitler lost the faith of the German people, he stayed confined in Berlin. On April 30, 1945, Hitler committed suicide by a gunshot to his head, which ended Nazi Germany. His wife of one day, Eva Braun, also took her life by taking Cyanide. In accordance with Hitler's prior written instructions, their bodies were doused in petrol and set alight in the garden outside the bunker.

The war was going badly, and defeat was imminent. Formal surrender documents were signed on September 2, 1945, ending World War II. It was six years and one day from the beginning of the war.

[1]End of World War II

— CHAPTER 4 —

AN OFFICER AND A GENTLEMAN?

In the days after the war, soldiers of the United States, France, Soviet Union, and Great Britain occupied West Germany. The United States emerged from World War II as a world superpower, challenged only by the USSR. The daily labor of rebuilding Karlsruhe, which lay in shambles, continued for many years. Now there was never any time for grieving, only surviving[1].

The port of Karlsruhe had a US Army base with a French garrison. I saw the town being occupied first by the French and then by the allied forces. When the French first occupied the town, the townspeople resisted, and for three days, there was pillage and strife. Whatever the French wanted, they took and gave nothing in return. When American soldiers replaced the French, it was as different as day and night. The Americans were traders, and when they wanted something, they were willing to pay for it.

Our lives were filled with the daily task of cleaning bricks from bombed-out homes and businesses so the city could use

---

3   www.wikipedia.org

them to rebuild. We worked to the point of exhaustion, scraping and cleaning each heavy brick. It was back-breaking work. I no longer dressed like a man but worked as hard as a man to rebuild my city. Dawn brought another problem of what to do with dead bodies littering our city. The sickly stench of cold decomposing bodies of friends, neighbors, and soldiers became our priority. The grim task of taking care of this problem forced Mama and me, along with others, to perform the removal and burial of the corpses. It was easier if we did not think of them as people at all. We all stole from their bodies without any sign of remorse as we put them in mass graves.

Tension between Mama and me began to build as one weary day followed another with no relief in sight. One night I had enough. I screamed at Mama, "I cannot keep doing this; I will not."

"What are you talking about? Ida, this is your duty to your country! How dare you talk like this?" She looked at me with astonishment.

"Mama, you might be able to continue with this horrible life, but I want something better for my life." It took all my courage to face her disapproval.

Mama's disapproval was obvious as she turned to walk away, saying, "This saddens me beyond words. Do not speak of this again!"

From that day on, I began to dream of going to the United States of America. I wanted to escape from the ruins of Germany. I needed to come up with a plan to get enough money to leave and go to the United States. I knew I could get money from soldiers if I gave them what they wanted. This time I could entertain soldiers on my terms. I would give them what they wanted only if I could exchange it for money, food, coffee, clothes, and cigarettes. Cigarettes were free for the American soldiers. All these goods were nearly impossible for civilians to obtain. I was good at bartering or selling goods for a nice profit.

Hilda and I had many discussions about our secret indiscretions with so many soldiers. She blurted out, "Ida, you know we have to be careful about being seen with American soldiers. Things are hard enough without getting our friends' or our family's disapproval for fraternizing with the soldiers."

"I no longer care what others think. I'm going to get out of this country one way or another," I replied. "Are you with me or not?"

"You're dreaming if you think it's possible for us to get to the United States, and besides, I cannot leave my family, and I do care what others think."

"I will get to the United States, and I will bring Mama over after I'm settled. I'm going to do whatever it takes. You stay if you must."

After this conversation, I was more determined than ever. I realized that I had power over men. I entertained many soldiers but eventually developed a serious relationship with an American soldier, Staff Sergeant Arnold Arnett, and a French officer,

Francois Monet. During my dates with Arnold, he continually bragged about his lavish home and the rich lifestyle he enjoyed in America. He often brought me presents of goods that I was unable to get as a German citizen. While I enjoyed Arnold's attention and gifts, I felt no emotional attachment to him; however, I soon began to think that he might be my ticket to the United States. I kept my relationships with all other soldiers confidential and strictly business.

At night, I tossed and turned, reliving the nightmare of the violent stripping of my innocence. Shame convinced me that I was unworthy to be loved. The torment of guilt, the pain of the haunting memories by the soldier and priest, and the death of my newborn son robbed me of any sleep. It only deepened the conviction that I was not capable of loving anyone or that anyone could ever love me. I became more and more obsessed with getting to the United States and away from war-torn Germany and the nightmares of my past. I believed that in the United States, all my troubles would be behind me.

As the months passed, the liaison with my young, handsome French officer, Francois, became more and more passionate. My lonely heart began to awaken with thoughts of the kind of love that I had only dreamed about as an innocent young girl. Francois took his time with his affection and tender expressions of love, which awakened desires in me that I had never felt before. His gentle touch as he caressed my body made me feel cherished. My rendezvous was different with Francois, who became my favorite lover. Gradually, I realized that I was falling passionately in love with my handsome French officer. I now longed for our times together. He charmed me with his words and his wit. He offered me a glimpse of a better life. One of the gifts Francois gave me was a fur coat. I had never been given a gift so expensive.

Francois would say, as he held me in his arms, "Darling Ida, just tell me what you want. You are so beautiful. I love you, and I want to make you happy."

I looked into those deep blue eyes and lovingly replied, "You do make me happy, just being with you, Francois. If only my heart could tell you how much I love you. My words are not enough. I do not want anything but you, my love," I would answer.

"I am wealthy, my darling, and I can give you whatever you want."

"The only thing I want is for you to stay with me tonight." Spending the night with Francois would turn out to be a life-altering decision. Sadly, I knew that Francois would never give me the one thing I had to have—a ticket to the United States. He would soon be returning to France, which I reasoned offered me very little of the future I wanted. France was also recovering from the devastation of the war. I wanted no part of rebuilding another country.

In the early summer of 1947, I found out I was pregnant. Francois and I had spent too many nights lying in each other's arms after making love, so I knew the father was Francois. The problem was he could not get me or my baby to the United States.

I decided to tell Arnold that my baby was his, hoping that the American soldier would marry me and take me with him to the United States. My choice meant that I had to leave my beloved Francois behind. It was a heart-wrenching decision, but my future depended on my getting out of Germany. I knew of other girls who had trapped American soldiers by getting pregnant, so they could get to the United States, so I believed I could do the same. It was weeks before I saw Arnold again. I had planned over and over in my mind what I was going to say, but now I only felt panic. I had to shake the fear and make him believe the lie. I hoped he would marry me so he would take me, and later, Mama, to the United States.

That night, Arnold met me at the Karlsruhe Pyramid at the town square. When he arrived, he embraced me, holding me in his arms. I hoped that Arnold would not notice my shaky hands. I decided that tonight was the right time to convince Arnold to believe my act of deception. I sweetly said, "Arnold, I have something to tell you." Arnold looked into my eyes expectantly. "I'm pregnant," I said, looking for the expression on his face.

A smile lit up his face. "This is great news!" He was very excited. He grabbed me and held me in his arms. *He's delighted!* I thought. *This is too good to be true.* "Does your mama know?" he asked, still smiling.

"I plan on telling her tomorrow night." I was thrilled at his response to the news.

"I want to be with you when you tell her," he insisted.

"No, I must tell her alone," I pleaded.

Arnold blurted out, "Marry me! I love you, and I want you to return with me to the United States. You'll have a wonderful life!" He had agreed to marry me; this was just what I wanted. My dream could come to pass. I could not even answer. I just started crying, which he thought was my reaction to his proposal. As I turned to leave, Arnold reached out and held me close and whispered in my ear, "Now you will be mine forever!"

The next day I rehearsed the words I would use to tell Mama, words that would change my life. That night in my home above the cafe, I decided it was now or never. I had to tell Mama about my pregnancy. I knew I would have to have help this time when my baby came. As we sat down to supper, I picked at my food. My nervousness at having to tell Mama destroyed my appetite. I had no idea how she would receive my news. She did not seem to notice that I was not eating. "Mama, I want to tell you something." She looked at me with a curious look on her face. "I have been seeing an American soldier named Arnold Arnett."

"What do you mean by seeing?"

"I am pregnant, and I told him last night that he is the father of my baby."

"Is he the father? I know you've been keeping company with a number of soldiers."

"Mama, that is my business, not yours."

"What did he say?" she snapped.

"He wants to marry me and take me to the United States!"

Mama looked startled. "You cannot leave your family now that you're going to have a baby! This will be my first grandchild. You cannot deny me this child."

"Have I not told you all along that I want a better life? Do not try to stop me," I demanded.

"I guess you have already decided." She got up out of her chair with a disdainful look on her face and began to clear the dishes from the table. I attempted to help her, but she snatched the plate from my hand. It would take time for her to absorb my news. I knew the best way to handle Mama was to leave her alone to work things out in her own mind. I quietly went into my bedroom and softly closed the door.

The next morning, when I came out of my bedroom, Mama was sitting on the couch in deep thought. She looked toward me and said, "I have decided to help you when the time comes for you to have your baby."

I nervously said, "Thank you, Mama! Arnold has promised me that he will bring you to the United States after we get settled."

"Let's not talk about that right now." Mama stood up from the couch with a skeptical look on her face and quickly left the apartment.

The morning of February 22, 1948, a midwife was brought to the flat to help deliver my baby. I lay on the couch in hard labor with a proper midwife and Mama at my side. There was no time for my stepfather, Hans, to find Arnold at his army base. The baby came so quickly that my newborn fell on the floor during the delivery. Everyone held their breath while they moved quickly to check to make sure the newborn was alive. This time I had a daughter. The baby was letting everyone know that she was alive and well.

The midwife swaddled my baby girl and laid her in my arms. As I looked at her tiny face, I thought of the birth of my baby boy. My grief turned to joy, and I determined that this time, my baby would make it. "I promise you; your life will be good in the United States." I softly hummed a lullaby to my precious daughter, Iris.

She was alive and well.

— Chapter 5 —

Land of Promise

Staff Sergeant Arnold Leroy Arnett had agreed to marry me. At one time, there was a ban on American soldiers marrying German girls due to the War Bride Act of December 28, 1945. That ban expired in December of 1946. The American soldiers' commanding officer still had to sign permission for any soldier to marry. Those who tried to enter the United States without proper military sponsorship could be sent back home.

Arnold was eleven years older than me and not as handsome as Francois. Arnold had dark brown hair with a high receding hairline and brown eyes, but he was my ticket to America and a better, prosperous life for me and my daughter.

Servicemen ignored the non-fraternization policy, and the military continued to place restrictions on such unions with at least a three-month waiting period and a careful screening before marriage. Staff Sergeant Arnett completed the application and paperwork then submitted it to his commanding officer. The wheels of the military turned slowly, but I was patient. It was seven months after the birth of my daughter when we finally received permission that we could marry and leave for the United States. When we married on September 7, 1948, I wore a beautiful black wedding dress, which was symbolic of elegance, class, and wealth. Little did I know what was ahead.

Mama, realizing that I was really leaving, kidnapped my baby to keep me from leaving Germany. She kept my daughter hidden so I could not find her. I was resentful and frantic and refused to live in the same apartment with Mama. I went to stay with Hilda. There were only two weeks left before our flight would leave for the United States.

One afternoon I was about to knock on Mama's apartment when my stepfather suddenly came out of the door. I whispered so Mama would not hear me, "Hans, please meet me this afternoon at the cafe downstairs." He looked at me suspiciously and quickly shook his head in agreement.

"I will be there at 2 p.m., but do not be late. I will not have much time, and your mother will be expecting me home."

I arrived at the cafe and waited anxiously at a table in the back, hoping that Hans would show. At last, Hans entered, looking around cautiously for me. He caught my eye, and I waved him to the table. "What do you want? Are you crazy? Your mama is jealous enough of you already. If she knows that we're meeting, I'll have her wrath to deal with."

"I have never asked anything of you before, but now I need you somehow to get my baby away from Mama and return her to me."

"I'll happily do whatever it takes to get you and this baby

out of our lives. Your mama is consumed with this child and keeping you in Germany. Give me some time, and I'll find a way."

"Thank you, Hans. You need to return her quickly. Arnold and I only have six days before we fly to the United States. I cannot miss this flight."

"I do not want you to miss it, either!" He turned to leave. He hesitated at the door and looked up and down the street to make sure Mama was not outside.

"Let me know where to meet you after you get my baby. I cannot thank you enough."

Two days passed as I waited in agony. *Will my stepfather be able to get my baby away from Mama?* After supper, Hilda and I heard a knock at her front door. When Hilda opened the door, a note fell off the doorknob onto the stoop. We both grabbed the note and cried as we read it out loud. "I will have your daughter at our apartment in the morning. You must be here at 10 a.m., and do not be late if you want your baby. *Viele Grube* (best regards), Hans."

Hilda and I hugged and wept, knowing that I would soon have my baby and leave for the United States.

I could hardly sleep, filled with anticipation, waiting for daylight. The next morning Arnold drove me to my parents' apartment. I asked him to wait in the car for me. I approached the door of Mama's apartment and quickly opened it. Hans stepped out from the bedroom and put his finger to his lips, gesturing for me to keep quiet. He had found my daughter.

"Your baby is asleep, and your mama has gone to the market to shop. She will not be away long, and I want you and this baby to be gone before she gets back." I quietly followed Hans into the bedroom and picked up my sleeping daughter. She awoke, looking up at me with a smile. "I'll help you carry your things down to your car, but then you're on your own."

"I'll never forget your help. Tell Mama I'll keep my promise." We hurried down the stairs where my husband, Arnold, was waiting. I looked back just in time to see Hans greeting Mama walking down the street toward him. He took the groceries from her arms and turned Mama toward the stairs. She had not seen our escape. We were safe to leave in the morning.

I had lost my son in my war-torn country. I was determined not to lose my daughter in Germany. My only hope was to get us to the United States. I had given my promise to Mama that I would bring her to the land of promise as soon as possible. I was determined to keep that promise.

The American Overseas Airlines, on October 3, 1948, left from Frankfurt, Germany, and arrived at New York International Airport in a drizzling rain. We flew over New York Harbor. Tears of joy filled my eyes and fell down my cheeks. I was in the land of my dreams! My joy was mixed also with the grief I was feeling, missing the love of my life, Francois Monet, and for having to leave Mama and Hilda behind. As the plane circled, I looked out the window and caught sight of the Statue of

Liberty on Bedloe's Island (later known as Liberty Island). The statue stood proudly in the harbor, welcoming immigrants and returning soldiers to the United States. I sobbed openly as we arrived in New York City.

My deception had come to fruition, and I had finally arrived in the United States of America. I left my homeland behind, and now I would be living in a foreign country. I did not know the language, but I had my American husband and my baby daughter.

I had survived World War II and Hitler's regime.

Part 2: Iris' Story

Proud to Be an American

World War II ended in 1945, and by 1949, over 20,000 German war brides had married American soldiers and emigrated to the United States. America's mood was very optimistic now that the war was over. Women were giving up their jobs to the returning men, even though they had tasted independence. These were exciting times now that families had turned the corner of depression. Wages were about $0.43 per hour, and the returning World War II veterans were offered benefits through the GI Bill for low-cost mortgages and education. Families had hope for the future.[1]

---

4   www.wikipedia.org

— CHAPTER 1 —
GRIT OR GRITS?

The young war bride, Ida, was my mother. This story is inspired by true events that Mama told me, I witnessed, or I was told by others who either loved or hated her.

I am that child she brought to the United States of America when she was twenty-five years old. She named me Iris Ruby Zubiller Arnett. This is *my story*. I was given American citizenship because of a *father* who enlisted on November 13, 1945, in the 48th Battalion of the United States Army. He was thirty-five years old when he brought us to America. I never knew until years later that my true biological father was a French officer, Francois Monet.

I had blond hair and blue eyes like my mother, Ida, and my biological father, Francois Monet. I was told by relatives who knew me as a young child that I was a happy and excitable child, full of love that reached out trustingly to any stranger I met. I woke up happy, and I did funny things to make others laugh. I was fearless, independent, outgoing, imaginative, strong-minded, and confident. I could do everything by myself; I did not need anyone's help. I could climb up on the kitchen counter to get whatever I wanted. I was never afraid of any danger and was curious about everything. I, too, had courage, which began to assert itself deeply within my German soul.

Arnold was born on September 10, 1912, in Mount Pleasant, Georgia, and was one of nineteen children. His parents were Arthur and Lottie Arnett, who lived in Auburndale, Florida, on a farm. Arthur Leroy Arnett, my grandfather, was a poor farmer who had a grit grinding mill. He used a mule to plow the field and drove a rusty old pickup truck that pulled a wagon to haul vegetables and fruit to town to sell. He had many other jobs. He drove a school bus and worked as a carpenter when needed.

My grandparents lived in a shabby, unpainted, two-bedroom mill house with an old, weathered tin roof. It was sparsely furnished. They had no electricity. They used oil lamps which only cast a small flickering light. They cooked on a wood-burning stove and heated their home with the fireplace. Grandma Lottie cooked and served three meals a day for the men who helped work in the corn and sugarcane fields. Syrup was made by grinding the sugar cane. Cows would provide milk which she churned into butter. Mom hated the grits that were served at almost every meal, but she ate them anyway without complaint. She showed unyielding courage in the face of their rejection. My mother had true grit.

Living was hard and demanding, especially when you are born into extreme poverty. In the evenings, the family spent their time listening to the radio. There were no luxury items like washing machines or refrigerators. All the clothes were washed by hand and none too frequently. To keep food cold, my grandfather would dig a hole three feet deep and two feet by two feet square, lining it with several burlap bags. He would then place a block of ice inside, add the food, cover it with more burlap bags, a piece of tin, and lastly, cover it with dirt. Grandfather also had a primitive, superstitious mind, making my cousins wear a dried mole's foot, tied in a tiny cloth bag, around their neck to ward off sickness or bad spirits. My grandfather drank daily from the brown bottle he carried in his pocket. He was an alcoholic and a womanizer, even though he was also a hard-working southern man.

I came to understand that my father had joined the army to escape from his family and his life of poverty and backbreaking work. The irony is, he was searching for a better life, just like Mama was, but instead of finding a better life, they both found abject poverty. My father's childhood home was clearly not the palatial home he had promised Mama. The fantasies he had created in Germany were all lies. America was the land of opportunity, but not for everyone, and surely not for us.

As the years passed, Mama discovered my father, like his father, was also an alcoholic and womanizer. Wherever she went, she heard the whispers and wagging tongues. She had to avoid certain people that my father owed money to, and there were many. Mom was homesick for her family and her homeland, Germany, and more disillusioned about America because of her life with my father.

The many visits to my father's family farm became more stressful for Mama. They had difficulty understanding her since she could only speak in her native tongue. They would laugh and mock her when she did attempt to speak English, especially when Mama proudly repeated the American curse words that she had learned from my father. The first time Mama saw their farm, she was in shock. I hated when we had to stay with them for any length of time. There was no inside bathroom, only the tar-papered, rickety, outdoor two-seater bathroom behind the chicken coop. I was afraid of the critters that I imagined lived around the smelly shack they called *the bathroom*. I never wanted to have to use the outhouse during the day, but after dark, it was even more terrifying. Dangling over a hole where any kind of scary animal might be lurking to jump up and grab me was a horrifying experience.

Eventually, Mama received letters from Germany sent to her by my grandmother, Oma, and Mom's best friend, Hilda. There was an economic miracle well underway. After the end of the war, productivity and living standards across West Germany were generally meeting or even surpassing pre-war levels. In her thoughts and dreams, Mom reflected on her past unbearable life in Germany. She yearned to fulfill her promise of bringing her mama to live in the United States without the means to do so.

My father had never planned on bringing her mama across the pond.

He was not a man of his word.

My father received his army orders to go to Augusta, Georgia, so once again, we had to move. My brother was born eight months later, on February 6, 1950, at the Oliver General Hospital in Richmond County, Georgia. They named him Arnold Leroy Arnett Jr. My father demanded that he have complete control of where Mama went and what she did every minute of every day. There could not be any doubt that Arnold Jr. was his son because he resembled my father and the only boy born that month.

On June 25, 1950, the Korean War broke out. My father received new army orders under the direction of the United Nations. His 48th Battalion was ordered to defend South Korea, which was fighting against North Korea. Mom, my baby brother Arnold Jr., and I were sent back to live with my grandparents, who lived in Auburndale, Florida. My father had nowhere else to leave his family while he served his country during the Korean War.

Living is hard and demanding when you are born into extreme poverty.

— CHAPTER 2 —
DEAD MAN WALKING

In Florida, it was an extremely hot, humid summer. Across the world in South Korea, my father was facing the opposite temperatures of an extreme below-zero cold. Thousands of soldiers like himself suffered frostbite. How do you face another day or even an hour and keep your sanity in a war that has no mercy? Even the weather was their enemy.

My father often wrote to Mama about how he lived each day, waiting to receive a letter from her and his family so that for a few minutes, he could escape the loneliness, fear, and pain all around him.

It was on his birthday, September 10, 1951, at an army camp in South Korea, that Master Sergeant Arnold Leroy Arnett finished his lengthy love letter to Mom. It was written on fifty-six feet of rolled paper, and he had used an undetermined quantity of ink just to say "happy anniversary" to his German-born wife, Ida. It had taken him three days to complete the letter. He then mailed it to Mama in the States. She had to get someone to interpret the letter for her. The special letter was even copied and then published on the front page of the *Lakeland Florida*

Ledger, featuring the long-distance love affair of an American soldier for his beautiful young German wife. Would this public display of love for his German-born wife be a foretelling of a lasting marriage? *The Lakeland Ledger* newspaper also sent a reporter to interview my mother. He asked, "How are American children different from German children?"

She replied through an interpreter, "Here you ask a boy what he wants to be, and he says, 'A cowboy,' and they play baseball and football. In Germany, the boys played war. They pretended they were fighting the Russians and there would be street wars."

Later my father was caught by his commanding officer committing unspeakable acts in the Korean War. He was given a medical discharge under dishonorable conditions from the US Army. He did remain eligible for VA Benefits such as health care and education. My father was forced to return to the States to his discontented wife and two young children. He was unemployed, suicidal, and humiliated by the acts he had committed. That life choice would change our lives.

During my childhood, I often overheard my father talking with his army buddies about the North Koreans sacrificing their children as weapons. They knew that the American soldiers were compassionate towards Korean children. The Koreans would strap hidden hand grenades on the children and send them into the army camps. As the soldiers innocently approached a child, reaching to give them candy, the hand grenades would detonate, killing the soldiers and the children. Many of my father's army buddies were killed by this brutal North Korean tactic. The humiliation of his army discharge seemed to cause the light that was once inside him to go dark. He became a dead man walking. Mama's dream of coming to America continued to evolve into a lifeless dark nightmare.

She wrote a letter to Hilda confiding her troubled thoughts, *Will I ever see Mama again? How am I going to survive in America? I have a husband who does not have a job, that I have never truly loved, and who promised me so much but gave me nothing in return.* Hilda did not respond to Mom's questions. Of course, she had already warned Mom about coming to America. There was not much else for Hilda to say except, "I told you so."

My father could not live with his shame and disgrace. After returning from Korea, he brought us back to Augusta, Georgia. He was trying to take what was wrong and make it right.

He did not have the power to make things right for himself or our family.

— CHAPTER 3 —
SHAME HAS A VOICE

One night my father came home from a drunken night out with his buddies, ranting and raving. He came in looking for a fight, stumbling, knocking over the lamp, as he yelled, "Why are those kids still awake?" Mom rushed Arnold Jr. and me toward our bedroom door. We all knew what was coming. I started to shake. I buried my head in my mama's skirt, crying. Mama moved us quickly into our bedroom and locked the door. He yelled, "You better open this door!"

"Arnold, just go to bed. I'll be there in a minute," Mama pleaded.

We were all terrified as he kicked the door open into our bedroom. He grabbed me, pulled me to himself, reached behind his back, pulling a gun from his waistband. He put the gun to my temple while yelling at Mom, "I'm going to kill her and you next!"

Using a soothing voice, Mother said, "No, no, *mein liebling* (my darling), put the gun down. Why are you so upset? You know you do not want to kill us. Let me put the children to bed." Mama slowly moved towards my father and said seductively, "Please *liebling*, go into our bedroom. I will make you feel better tonight." as she gently pulled me from him. She was able to convince my father to diffuse his anger. He lowered the gun and left the room.

He would often threaten to kill us and himself. I was no longer a happy child full of love and confidence but became a child consumed with terrifying fear and low self-esteem. I feared the dark because that was when I saw and heard my parents fighting. I hated him for what he was doing to our family. Night meant that we might die by the hand of an alcoholic father who should have been protecting us.

Whenever Mom heard my father's car pull into the driveway, she would force us to run to meet our father in his car, hoping that his own children could put him in a better mood before he came into our apartment. He liked to appear to others as a charming, kind, loving veteran and father. He kept candy in his pockets to hand out to neighborhood children who would also meet him as he got out of his car. They lifted their hands in the air, giggling for the candy and his loving embrace. No one knew the real man he was behind closed doors.

The year was 1954, and I was almost seven years old. One afternoon I was playing with other children at the park across from our rented apartment. We all left the park as I quickly headed home to use the bathroom. As I walked down the sidewalk, there was a car with a man sitting alone on the passenger side. He called out, "Hey, little girl, come here. What is your name?" I innocently came closer.

"My name is Iris." In those days, I was not warned to never speak to strangers. I would often wake to find strangers who had spent the night on our sofa in our home. No one even locked their front doors before going to bed. Then I noticed he was sitting in the car with his pants down to his knees, pleasuring himself. He clearly wanted me to watch. I stood by his car, frozen with fear, tears streaming down my face. He stopped and quickly pulled up his pants, holding them with one hand. He got out of the car, grabbed my arm, and forced me into the nearby woods. I was crying and shaking with horror. No one was around to see or hear me. He led me into the bushes, where he lifted my dress and tore my undergarments off and began touching me while he dropped his pants. I was so terrified I felt pee run down my legs into my new shoes. He took a step away from me toward a bush to relieve himself. I knew now was my chance to run as fast as I could to get to my home. I ran so fast I fell in the middle of the road across from our apartment.

When I got home, I was crying my heart out; my knees were bleeding from the fall. Mama thought I was crying over my bloody knees. I blurted out my story about the stranger. She saw that I had wet myself, and the shoes she had bought me at the thrift store were filled with pee. I thought she was going to call the police as she had on my father many times when he was drunk and beating one of us. Domestic abuse was common in our house. Instead, she grabbed me angrily by the hand, and out the door we went to find this stranger she believed I had made

77

up. Mama walked me back across the street to find the stranger I had just told her about. His car was no longer parked at the curb. He was nowhere to be found.

Instead of Mama believing and comforting me, she was now convinced of what she had first suspected—that I had made it all up. My father had recently threatened to whip me with his belt if I wet myself again, saying I was too old to still be wetting my underwear. My problem was, I never wanted to stop having fun playing long enough to stop and go inside to the bathroom. I would wait too long to make it and would wet my panties. Ironically, this time I had been trying to get home to go to the bathroom. Mama believed that I had made up the story to keep from being punished and that I had thrown my wet panties away to hide the evidence. She sent me to the bedroom for lying, announcing that I would not be able to come out till my father got home to spank me. How would a child know how to make up sexual abuse without being sexually abused? My trust in my parents was badly damaged. I began to believe that I was a bad child deserving to be abused.

As I look back now, I believe that the sexual abuse incident in the park, coupled with my parents' disbelief, convinced me that there was no point in telling anyone about any abuse that I would encounter. If my own parents did not believe me, what were the chances anyone else would believe me? I also accepted the shame, blame, and guilt for an act I had no control over. This pattern of shame would become a struggle which I would have to fight to overcome for most of my adult life. I came to know, *"shame" has a voice. It could speak to me whenever it wanted.*

Shame was a voice louder than any sound of happiness or contentment.

— CHAPTER 4 —
THE HIDING PLACE

My father began moving us from one city to another and from one job to another. He was out of the army, but the army was not out of him. Whenever my father moved us, he would only take what he could pack in the car. He left everything else. Even our favorite toys were given to the neighborhood children or left on the street curb for anyone to take. Carpentry was the only trade he knew, so we went wherever he could find work. We were still living in extreme poverty in Georgia. Mom despised the south and their southern food and sweet tea. She did not understand their southern drawl and did not like the slow-paced lifestyle. Mama longed for the fast-paced and more exciting life of the big city of New York, where she had met other immigrants like herself during the short time we had lived there.

New York City had a Germantown. She pleaded with my father to move us back to New York City. My father hated the big city, so he decided to compromise by moving us to Paterson, New Jersey. We were close enough for her to visit the big city, but also where he knew he could find a job as a carpenter. Paterson, back in the 1950s, was an exciting place to live.

My brother, Arnold Jr., was five, and I was seven. My memories of those days were of my father and mother drinking and fighting. The bitter cold winters would lock us in our home for days, making us unable to get outside but for a short time. We lived in an attic which the landlord had converted to an apartment. It was a small and cramped two-bedroom apartment with ceilings that were low and slanted. The apartment was dark and gloomy, with windows on each end. I would sit in our bedroom on the window seat high above the street, watching people pass by. In the winter, I loved to watch out of my window as the snow fell. The snow was beautiful as it covered the dirty streets and made them look clean. It also brought the task the next day of having to help my father shovel the sidewalk in front of the house so he could get his car out to go to work. He was a harsh disciplinarian with a fiery temper. I would use my vivid imagination to daydream of being in another place.

I was asleep in my bed when my father loudly slung open the door of our bedroom, waking me. He pulled me out of my bed and pushed me to my favorite window seat. He whispered, "Do not wake your brother. Watch your mother getting out of that car." I could smell the alcohol on his breath. Mom was coming home late on a Friday night from her work as a waitress at a Delicatessen across town. A car slowly pulled up to the front of our apartment; an unfamiliar man had driven her home. He helped Mama out of the car, and they began caressing each other under the streetlight. I guess she thought my father was asleep or passed out, to be so bold. I was scared because I knew there was going to be another fight when she walked up the long flight of stairs into our apartment. I began crying; my father slapped me across the face while slurring his words, "Stop that crying! See, that is how you will turn out! A no-good tramp! You will never amount to anything." He only stopped hitting me when he heard Mama's heels coming up the stairs. I ran to meet her at the door, but he pushed me out of his way.

As Mama entered through the door, she looked startled when she saw my father in a rage, waiting for her. He grabbed her by her hair and slammed her against the wall. I could hear her holding her own, fighting back the best way she could, as I ran terrified, covering my ears with my hands to drown out the sound of violence. Convinced I would be the next one he would turn his anger toward, I slid into the corner of my bedroom closet, where I often escaped. I quietly closed the door behind me, trying to drown out the sound of their fighting. The darkness consumed me while I hid, covering my mouth so as not to be heard while I softly cried in terrifying fear until I fell asleep.

I woke up early the next morning, still in the closet, to a silent house. Terrifying fear flooded my heart once again. I was afraid to come out of the closet. To this day, I cannot be in a closed room with no windows without an uncontrollable feeling of panic. I did not know what I would find after last night's drama. This kind of event was becoming a weekly occurrence, and there was no way of escape. I quietly and slowly opened the door, peeking out to make sure no one was awake. I focused on getting dressed; then I woke up my brother, Arnold Jr. "Get dressed and hurry up. Be very quiet," I whispered.

It was Saturday morning, which meant no school. We left quietly without any breakfast, carrying our shoes so my father would not hear us tiptoeing down the steps. Once outside, we put on our shoes and ran to a neighbor's home to play with their children. We often escaped to their home, never telling them that we were hiding from the mental anguish, *alcohol addiction*, and domestic violence that went on in our home. They would insist that we join their family for breakfast. We were escaping, if only for a short time, into a family's home that had love and laughter. I would look around the table and dream of having a mother and father like them, but the dream never lasted long. The dreaded phone call would come telling them to send us home.

My father sank deeper into depression while Mama became more independent and more determined than ever for us to escape from him. She secretly earned money as a part-time hairstylist for the ladies who lived in the neighborhood. She planned on saving enough to take us and leave him. My father insisted Mama only speak English, especially when he was at home. She would only speak to us in her native tongue, German, when my father wasn't around. Mama desperately wanted to escape from my father's control.

Mother was not living the American Dream.

— CHAPTER 5 —
CALIFORNIA OR BUST

Mama was very beautiful to me. She would whisper, "I can make more tips, Iris, than the other girls at work because I know how to get men to do what I want." She bragged that she could always get a man to bring her home after work. "I do not have to pay to ride the city bus." She smiled. She could also pocket the small bus fare my father gave her to add to her hidden savings for us to escape.

One snowy night when we were at our friend's home, my father called and insisted that we come home. As we walked down the street to our apartment, I could see the backseat of our car was already packed with our clothes. I entered the apartment nervous because I suspected we were leaving again. Father said, "You both need to get ready. We are leaving tonight to move to California." Arnold Jr. looked at him with eyes of excitement. He picked him up and said, "This will be a great adventure, Arnold. We will have fun, and I promise that we will live in a house by the ocean." We never lived in nor owned a house. His promise of a better life was supposedly waiting for us in California.

I asked, "Where is Mama?"

He snapped, "Your mother will follow this weekend after she finishes working."

"Where in California?" I questioned.

He responded, "Oakland, California."

"I do not want to go without Mama. Let's just wait till she is finished work and leave on Monday. I pleaded.

"That is enough with your questions, do not say another word. Take your brother and get in the car now!" he angrily responded. "I already have a good job just waiting for me! Let's go. There isn't any room in the car for anything else. Your mother will bring the rest when she comes."

I begged again, "Oh, please, let's wait for Mama to come home from work. I want to see her and leave in the morning, not tonight."

He began screaming, "Do you want a spanking? I said get in the car." I was terrified as he forced us into his car. We crawled into the back seat on top of our clothes, piled high, hugging one another. We left in the cold dark night traveling to Oakland, California, in the winter of 1955.

My father was kidnapping us from our mother, and we had no idea of his devious plans. We were also leaving our friends and the safe haven of the family that lived two doors down. Years later, Mama told me that my father had found her hidden money and realized what she was planning. He decided to take her money and leave her first. He took my brother and me to punish her. Mama told me that she came home to find a note from my father that read: *You will never see any of us again. If you call the police, I will kill Iris and Arnold then come back to kill you.*

My mother had to be sedated for several days, unable to work after finding us gone. She was terrified that she would never see us again. Mother knew he could kill her, Arnold Jr., and me. Mama never called the police as he demanded.

She was left alone, afraid, with no family and no money.

— CHAPTER 6 —

CHILDREN SHOULD
BE SEEN, NOT HEARD

It only took three and a half days to drive to Oakland, California, because my father drove day and night. He only stopped a few times to stock up on food; and several times, long enough to catch a few hours of sleep. When we had to go to the bathroom, my father would stop the car on the side of the road. He would then open the front and back doors where we had to stand, between the doors, and use the bathroom on the side of the road. My father was still uncertain that Mama would not call the police about us being kidnapped. He refused to allow us to be seen by anyone who might report our whereabouts.

Once, he stopped at a service station and went inside to pay for gas. I realized I could use the bathroom rather than the side of the road. I quickly jumped out of the back seat of the car, leaving my brother sleeping as I ran to use the station bathroom. My father returned to the car and, without looking back, sped away, leaving me at the gas station. When I came out of the bathroom, I saw that the car was gone. I panicked and ducked back into the bathroom until I could figure out what to do. I did not know what city or state I was in or who to call to get help, so I hid, crying in the bathroom stall. My father finally realized I was not in the car and turned around and came back to the gas station. He was furious as he entered the women's bathroom, pulling me by my hair out of the stall and beating me with his belt for leaving the car.

He carried two water bags strapped on the front bumper of the car so that when the car overheated in the desert, he could stop and add water. When the car cooled down, we would get back on the road. It was amazing that the old car made it to California. When we arrived, we stayed with his army buddy, Jack, in Alameda until my father rented an apartment in Oakland, California. We all slept on the floor for months until he could afford to slowly buy some furniture. My brother and I slept in the same twin bed. One of us slept with their head up at the headboard while the other faced the other direction with their head at the foot of the bed. There was no rest, peace, or joy in our home.

When Mama did not come to California as he had promised, my father changed his story. He told us she had left him for another man. My brother and I cried inconsolably, grieving for Mama and feeling betrayed and abandoned. Back in New Jersey, Mama once again turned to prostitution to survive. It provided for her very well. She was able to live in a penthouse suite, making an incredible amount of money working for the mafia, an organized crime family. When my father kidnapped us, he had taken all of Mama's hidden money and left her with nothing except her determination to survive. One of her clients brought my mother to the mafia. It was the number one organized crime family. They quickly became her family and protected her when she could no longer protect herself. She ran a prostitution ring for the syndicate, dealing with politicians, attorneys, doctors, and the so-called elite of society. Mama had beautiful clothes, furs, jewelry, and fancy cars. She traveled the world in the arms of some of her best clients.

My father always feared we would one day escape from him. He was able to keep in touch with his buddies back in New Jersey, who spied on Mama for him. He thought we would run to Mama if we found out about the wealthy lifestyle she was living. Of course, he also threatened he would kill us if we did try to escape. I knew no way of escape. There was no one that I could go to who would listen, even if I tried to tell someone what was going on in our house. We were constantly beaten on our heads, backsides, or anywhere he could keep it from showing in order that no one would see the bruises and scars. The hatred of his own life was spewed out on us. My father often repeated his mantra, "You'll never amount to anything; you made your bed now lie in it; children should be seen, not heard, and how you feel doesn't matter." Once an excitable and talkative child, I became shy and withdrawn.

On two different nights, I woke up and smelled smoke. I yelled for my brother to get out of the house. I ran through the house only to find that the smoke was coming from the mattress my father was passed out on. He had come home in his drunken stupor, passed out in his bed, and dropped his cigarette onto his mattress. I put the fire out both times, but I was terrified about what might happen if I did not wake up the next time there was a fire. *Would we all be burned alive in the apartment? Would my father's dark, hideous secrets ever be exposed? Would no one know about the horror we were living and the evil monster he had become?* I longed to be saved from our nightmare.

I knew I had to start sleeping with my father to protect my brother and myself. I had to become a mother to my younger brother and a wife to my father. Now that I was sleeping with my father in his bed, he began treating me like one of his women and would use me for his own satisfaction. My father had started molesting me gradually from the early age of seven. He had insisted that I sit with him in his chair in the living room. At first, his touch was playful, making me laugh. Tickling then turned to inappropriate touching. When it began feeling wrong, I would pull away. As time went on, he became more aggressive and determined to get his pleasure at my expense. Drunk or sober, my father steadily increased his evil acts from physical and emotional abuse to include sexual abuse.

My innocence was taken away from me. I could no longer look anyone in the eye. I could only stare at the floor when someone spoke to me. I was filled with shame, believing what was happening to me was somehow my fault.

My innocence was stolen from me.

— CHAPTER 7 —
LITTLE BLACK BOOK

My father was at work, and Arnold Jr. was sleeping when someone knocked on our door. My father had forbidden us to open the door when he was not at home, but for some reason, that morning, I opened the door. A strange man was standing on the front stoop. "Hello. Is your mother at home?" he asked.

"She's sick and cannot come to the door," I lied.

"I'm David from the church downtown. We're having Vacation Bible School next week. Our church bus will be in your neighborhood every morning to pick up any children who want to attend." He handed me a flier. "Please give your mother this flier with all the dates, time, and information. We will have fun activities, games, and prizes for anyone that comes. If you want to come, all you must do is be at the front of your house by 8:30 a.m. each morning, and the bus will pick you up. We'll bring you back home by noon. Oh, and here's a Bible, just for you. Have a great day. I will be praying for your mother to be well. I do hope we will see you at Vacation Bible School!"

I closed the door and looked at the little black book in my hand. I was excited and wanted to go to Vacation Bible School. How could I go? I opened the book to see what kind of book it was. The first thing I saw was a picture of a man with long hair dressed in a white robe who was sitting on a rock, surrounded by children. I knew I had to hide the book from my father. He would be enraged that I had opened the door and taken the flier and the black book from a stranger when he was not home. After that day, I would close the door of my bedroom and read this black book. I could not understand all the words but reading them somehow gave me peace and helped me to escape from my empty, lonely life.

I would often stand my doll and stuffed animals against the wall and read the black book out loud to them. One afternoon I did not hear the door open, nor did I realize that my father was standing in the doorway watching me loudly, reading the book as if I was preaching to them. He was infuriated. "Where did you get this Bible?" He snatched it out of my hand.

"I found it on the porch," I lied so I would not face his temper for opening the door.

"You do not need to be reading this junk. This will not help you. You do not understand it, anyway!" he bellowed as he left the room with my black book. I never saw it again.

On Sunday afternoons, my father would drive us around to his construction sites to show us the houses he was building. He dangled the promise of getting us our own home. Instead, we moved from apartment to apartment when we were evicted because he did not pay the rent. Often when we moved, we would be living in a new school zone. We had to start over in a new school so many times. We had no social skills. The teacher would begin, "Students, this is Iris Arnett. Please stand, Iris, and tell the class where you moved from and where you were born." I would timidly say, "I moved from New Jersey, but I was born in Germany." My classmates then labeled me a Nazi. They began their bullying. "Iris is a Nazi!" They taunted me every time they saw me. They also harassed me, making fun of how skinny and shy I was. I did not attempt to find a friend. They believed all Germans were Nazis.

From these experiences, I learned that telling the truth did not benefit me. Lying proved to be more beneficial. At the next school, I lied about being born in Germany. I lied about my mother, telling them she was dead. I never told anyone that she was alive, and she lived in New Jersey as a high-paying prostitute, which our father reminded us of every day. I lied that my father was the town drunk, even though he wore that label proudly. I was good at lying and lying became easier and more acceptable and less painful. Lying was better for me than telling the truth. If my lips were moving, I was lying. I was learning to survive in any way I could.

Today, teachers are held legally accountable if they do not report suspected child abuse from any of their students. Would my childhood have been different if a teacher had recognized that I was being abused? I was never taught when and how someone touches you could be wrong, nor how to report sexual advances. You also accept "shame" that you are tormented with, and the idea of having to tell someone what you have participated in was unthinkable. I knew I could never get away from my father because he would find me and kill me. I could not handle the guilt of wanting him to do exactly that...but I was torn because I did not want him to kill my brother or mother, so I stayed. You are rewarded just enough so that you begin to enjoy the moments of reward, enough to endure the pain, so you become hardened to abuse. A child deeply wants and needs to trust a parent. Imagination is so vivid that the captor plays on it to manipulate you and keep control over you. I promised myself if I ever got away from him, no man would ever abuse or control me again. I became convinced that this life I was living would be better than the unknown life I would have if I returned to my mother. I believed that if I went to the police, they would not give us back to Mama but take us to a judge who would put us in foster care.

My father would tell me that people do not really want to hear you air any dirty laundry. You would be exposing your part in participating in the sexual acts. He paraded around announcing that he was an American soldier who fought for this country, and people would believe him over my story. I knew nothing at the time of his disgrace from the army. It was his way of manipulating me to get what he wanted.

In a book written by Gavin de Becker in 1997 entitled: *The Gift of Fear, Survival Signals that Protect Us from Violence*[1], the author explains the dynamics of learned helplessness.

The way circus baby elephants are trained demonstrates this dynamic well: When young, they are attached by heavy chains to large stakes driven deep into the ground. They pull and yank and strain and struggle, but the chain is too strong, the stake too rooted.

One day they give up, having learned that they cannot pull free, and from that day forward, they can be chained with a slender rope. When this enormous animal feels any resistance, though it has the strength to pull the whole circus tent over, it stops trying. Because if it believes it cannot, then it cannot

You'll never amount to anything; you cannot sing; you're not smart enough; you're a loser; you should have more realistic goals; you're the reason our marriage broke up. Without you children, I'd have had a chance. You're worthless. This opera is sung in homes all over America right now; the stakes driven into the ground, the heavy chains attached, the children reaching the point they believe they cannot pull free. And at that point, they cannot..

Unless and until something changes their view unless they grasp the striking fact that they are tied with a thread, that the

———

5. Boston: Little Brown, pages 228-229

chain is an illusion, that they were fooled, and ultimately, that whoever so fooled them was wrong about them and that they were wrong about themselves—unless all this happens, these children are not likely to show society their positive attributes as adults.

I learned that when you criticize your children, they don't stop loving you; they stop loving themselves.

Eventually, my mother discovered where we were living through school records. Mama found us living in Oakland, California. Determined to get us back, she begged my father to allow us to have contact with her after she moved to California. When she arrived, my father reluctantly let Mama stay in our apartment, but only during the day while he was at work, and it was summer break from school. She rented a small room in a house nearby where she spent the nights. Mama was desperately trying to reconnect with my brother and me, but we still believed my father's lie that she had left us for another man. We were traumatized and distraught. We believed that she had decided to abandon us for another man and did not come to protect us from our father.

Mama took a job working at a dance hall where the men would buy tickets to dance with the girls. She made good tips because she gave them more than the dance on the floor. One afternoon Mama was off work, and we were riding our bikes when my brother went over the handlebars, crashing and nearly biting his tongue in half. Mom, in a panic, had a neighbor drive us to the emergency room. After that incident, my father would not allow Mama to see us without him, as if it was somehow her fault that my brother was a daredevil and had almost severed his tongue. He threatened to take her to court and convinced Mama that no court would give children to a prostitute. Mama grew weary and soon gave up the fight and returned to New Jersey and her mafia family.

My father received a phone call in the summer of 1960 that his younger brother, Bill, had been shot and killed by a jealous woman while he was working behind a bar. We traveled from California to Grandma Lottie's house for Uncle Bill's funeral in Auburndale, Florida. Instead of going back to California, we moved to Brunswick, Georgia, in the fall of 1960, so my father could be closer to his father. By this time, I was almost thirteen years old, and I was so full of rage and hatred toward my father. I was extremely rebellious and hard to handle. I began to defy my father and deny his sexual advances. I saw a glimmer of fear in his eyes on what I might do. He backed off some of his advances towards me and instead brought his strange women to stay overnight.

I started skipping school with my friend, Linda, so I could have some fun before I went to a house that was never a home. I smoked cigarettes that I kept hidden under a loose brick beneath the rented house that was built upon pillars. Linda was older than me. We stole my father's liquor bottles that he had not finished and drank the remainder. I often sneaked out of my bedroom window meeting Linda and her older boyfriend. My father never knew or cared when I went out or came in. Coming home meant I would find my father naked, either passed out on the floor or passed out in his bed, usually with a strange woman lying nude next to him. I discovered years later, he had married and divorced ten times for a total of nine wives (he married one woman twice) along with so many other women that he did not marry.

My father denied for years that he was an alcoholic. Now his body was suffering from years of alcohol abuse. The Veterans Administration doctor told him that his alcoholism was destroying his body. His diagnosis was inflammation of the liver and the lining of his stomach. When he passed out from his drunken binge, he would wake up in a pool of blood. The VA doctors warned him that he had to choose to stop drinking or choose to die. Even the truth of his condition did not motivate him to change.

The chain is an illusion.

— CHAPTER 8 —
SLEEPING WITH STRANGERS

My father eventually grew tired of Arnold Jr. and me and did not want to deal with us anymore. He asked his father, our grandfather, for advice on what to do. My grandfather was caretaking land that Mr. Dalton Hayes owned, and he often heard him talking about him and his wife wanting to have a child. My father had decided to leave Arnold Jr. with them for a weekend as a trial visit, but they never sent him back to us. My father finalized arrangements with Dalton and Louree Hayes to keep Arnold Jr. in their home with the promise of adoption after a year. I never knew if my father talked them into paying him for my brother. Mr. Hayes owned and operated Hayes Construction, a successful and prosperous construction company in Brunswick, Georgia.

My father and grandfather refused to tell me where they had taken my brother because they knew I would fight to get him back. I was heartbroken. He was all I had, and I loved him dearly. I was more than his sister; after all, I was his mother. My brother, at the age of eleven, moved into his new home on December 7, 1961. Mr. and Mrs. Dalton Hayes changed Arnold

Jr.'s name to Franklin Marcus De Hayes, and they affectionately called him Mark. The first year he lived with them, they wanted to instill a sense of discipline in him. Some of the summer months, he attended Riverside Military Academy in Gainesville, Georgia, then in the winter months, he attended Military Academy in Hollywood, Florida.

My father could not find a home for me even though he dragged me to many of his siblings, begging them to take me into their home. No one wanted to take on a rebellious teen. He was frustrated with the process of finding someone to take me off his hands. He would not even consider allowing me to live with my mother. He was still bitter, and angry with Mom, and jealous of her rich lifestyle.

One of my painful memories was when my father reluctantly took me to the home of his sister, Margaret. My father left me in the living room while they went into her kitchen. I knew they were going to be talking about me. I was determined to hear what they were saying. I quietly sneaked to the kitchen doorway, being careful not to be seen. Leaning against the wall near the doorway, I peeked in. He was seated at the table with Aunt Margaret's back to me. I overheard my father trying to convince my aunt to move me into their home since they already had daughters, Reail and Diane, along with a son, Johnny.

My father pleaded, "Please, Margaret, you must take Iris into your home. I have no one else to ask." Suddenly my heart began racing; I felt my face flush.

I began to shake, and I felt sick to my stomach when I heard Aunt Margaret bitterly raise her voice, saying, "No, I will not bring Iris into my home. She will be no better than a tramp like her mother. I will not have her corrupting my daughters." I ran out of her house, slamming the door behind me.

It was not long before my grandfather arranged for me to live and work in Waynesville, Georgia, with his friend and hunting buddy, Lester Harrison, and his wife, Emma Belle. They were empty nesters now that their daughters, Frances, and Mary, were married and out of their childhood home. Grandfather heard they could use someone to help work in their country store and restaurant. They owned and operated Harrison Grocery Store and Gas Station on Highway 84. Also, next door was their coffee shop restaurant that served a southern menu of a choice of meat and three vegetables. At that time, Waynesville only had one yellow caution light on the two-lane Highway 84 across from the restaurant. I worked in the grocery store and coffee shop for $5 a week, and the remainder of my pay went towards my room and board. They asked me to call them Aunt Emma Belle and Uncle Lester, to which I happily agreed. They were quiet, good people who did not know how to show affection to me. Understandably, they did not know what to do for a dysfunctional teenager with unresolved bitterness and anger. Their daughters, Frances and Mary, were always extremely kind towards me.

I attended Nahunta High School in Nahunta, Georgia. Often at night, I would lie in bed unable to sleep, scared and lonely, finally crying myself to sleep. I was sleeping in a home with strangers. They did not have a legal arrangement because my father still wanted the final say on matters pertaining to me. I was fourteen when Uncle Lester gave me permission to drive his truck to deliver groceries to their customers who had placed their orders earlier in the week. I woke up excited on Saturday mornings, rushing out the door of Harrison Grocery Store. In one hand was my soda bottle, filled with peanuts, and the customer list in the other. I would deliver the groceries on Browntown Road through a cloud of dust on the dirt roads in Waynesville. I will forever be grateful that they took me into their home when they did not have to. It was a safe place, even though it would be short-lived. In this safe place, I began to emerge out of my dark place. I began to gain friends and succeed in school. I had even won second place for the high school beauty contest "Miss Nahunta High" and won "Best Personality" for my senior year.

My friends would sneak out with me at night to go riding in the truck on the only paved road through Waynesville. I drove fast as if I was in a hurry to get somewhere, but I really did not have anywhere to go. As we got closer to the railroad track, I would turn off the truck headlights as we looked intensely into the pitch dark, straining our eyes to see any train lights from any train coming down the railroad track. If we did not see any lights, I would speed even faster, laughing and shouting out the window, "Ten to one, nothing is coming!" Once, we barely missed an oncoming train because none of us had seen the lights on the track.

I found refuge in this town which was founded originally as a refuge for weary stagecoach travelers. The people of Waynesville, Georgia, were very forgiving to a dysfunctional teenager who had a lot of emotional needs.

I was not afraid to die; I was afraid to live.

— CHAPTER 9 —

MY BROTHER'S KEEPER

My father still refused to tell me where my brother was living. I had friends from school secretly searching for my brother. One of my friends finally found Arnold, Jr., living with Dalton and Louree Hayes. I called his home to speak with him. I was so excited and filled with such pride that I had found my little brother. I cried when he answered the phone. "Arnold, Arnold, is that you?" I asked.

"Who is this?" he snapped.

"It's Iris, your sister," I responded.

"Do not call me Arnold. That's not my name. My name is Franklin Marcus De Hayes. Call me Mark. I'm playing pool with my friends. Call me back later."

That evening, I called Arnold back. I could tell from his voice that he was not happy that I had found him. He did not want me to interfere with the good life he was now enjoying. I could hear the happiness in his voice when he talked about his new family. I was truly glad for him but jealous that I did not have a family. I reminded him of his past, and he needed to forget his past. He was not really rejecting me, even though it felt like he was. He was only rejecting our abusive past. After I hung up, I recalled all the horror in our past. I had tried to protect him from the things my father did during the night hours. I know he faced terrible abuse also; at that time, it was too shameful and painful for us to discuss.

A month later, I was called out of my classroom to go to the principal's office for a phone call. I was in no hurry as I slowly strolled down the hall towards the office because I knew it had to be my father calling again with some new drama. To my surprise, it was Albert Findig, Mr. Hayes' attorney.

He said in a solemn voice, "Iris, I am so sorry to have to tell you, but Dalton Hayes died this morning of a massive heart attack."

"Oh no, it cannot be true."

Mr. Findig replied, "You remember that Dalton was supposed to sign the adoption papers today? The tragedy is that he had a heart attack in his office. The adoption papers for Mark are still lying unsigned on his desk."

I burst into tears. "I could not believe that Mark had lost a truly kind, loving, and generous man who wanted to be his father."

Even though Mark was never adopted, he kept his new name and to this day is called Mark. Mr. Findig also called my father to give him the news that Mr. Hayes had died. When my father heard the news, he made a phone call to Mrs. Hayes and scheduled a visit to see Mark. He arrived in the Hayes' driveway and honked his car horn for Mark to come out to his car. Mark came out and spoke to our father through the opened car window. My father hastily said, "Well, what do you want to do? Stay or go? It does not matter to me."

Mark answered, "I'm not going anywhere, especially not with you. I plan to stay!" The conversation lasted about five minutes. My father drove away as fast as he had arrived in the circular driveway.

Mark had a difficult time adjusting to Mr. Hayes' death, and he quit school when he was in the tenth grade. Weeks later, he ran away when the juvenile probation officer showed up at their door to enforce his returning to school. Mark only knew of one place to run. With much regret, he knew he had to return to his father, who had moved to Jacksonville, Florida. Mark moved into Father's apartment, but he soon realized that life had not changed because he was still having drunken binges for days. Mark finally left him after only eight months, hitchhiking seventy-five miles back to Brunswick, Georgia. He slept hidden under a bridge for three weeks, not taking a bath and begging for money and food.

Someone told Mrs. Hayes that Mark was back in town, and he was living under a bridge. She went to convince him to come back home with her. Mark did not want to go back because her lifestyle had changed after Mr. Hayes had died. She was handling her grief with alcohol and strange men staying in their home. Mrs. Hayes promised Mark if he came back to her home, she would quit her drinking and stop bringing the men in and out of their home. She did quit drinking and lived up to her promise to Mark.

Mark's full story will be told by him, not me.

— CHAPTER 10 —

I SCREAM FOR ICE CREAM!

It was a hot, beautiful Sunday afternoon when Aunt Emma Belle gave me permission to go with my boyfriend, Frank, to get ice cream in Brunswick, Georgia. We had stopped for a red light, and Frank had his arm around me. I was looking at Frank, laughing at something he had said. Then I turned back and looked across the road at the car facing us. It was my father in his car, glaring at me with rage, waiting for the light to change. When the light changed to green, my father made a U-turn in the middle of the road, squealing his tires coming up behind us! "Frank, drive faster!" I responded.

"Why is that guy on our tail?" Frank replied.

"We've got to get away. That's my father," I screamed.

"We are not doing anything wrong. I'd like to meet him," Frank pleaded.

"You do not understand what my father will do to me and you!" I cried.

Frank could not understand why I was so frightened. We were just going out for ice cream. My father ran Frank's car off the shoulder of the road into the ditch. Frank stopped the car and opened his door. My father began yelling at Frank, "Stay in the car if you know what's good for you." He opened my door and grabbed me by my hair.

He dragged me toward his car as I screamed to Frank, "Go tell Aunt Emma Belle!"

My father raced to my grandfather's house without speaking a word. When we arrived, my father jerked his belt from his pants, pulled me out of his car, and began to beat me with his belt. My grandfather came out on the porch. "What is going on out here?"

My father cursed and yelled, "I just caught this tramp with a man I do not know. We got to find somewhere else to put her." They left me on the porch, shaking and crying uncontrollably. I was not allowed to come into the house as they discussed what to do with me now that I had committed the unpardonable sin.

They called around to see if they could find someone who would take me. They even called the police to see if they would put me in a home for troubled juveniles. The police told them if there was one living parent, they could not take me into the system; after all, I had not done anything illegal. My grandfather called Uncle Lester. "Lester, why did you allow Iris to go off with that boy?"

He replied, "Arthur, I did not know she had left with any boy. Where is Iris now?"

"Arnold and I have her. We are trying to find somewhere to

put her."

Uncle Lester interrupted him, "Wait, let her continue to stay with us, and I will see to it that Iris will not be riding in any other boy's car."

My grandfather reluctantly agreed, "All right, I will drop her off at your house tonight. Make sure Iris promises you that she will never go off in another boy's car again."

I had to promise Uncle Lester as if my promise would mean anything. I told them what they wanted to hear, not what I would do! I did not hear from my father for a few weeks when one night, the doorbell rang at Uncle Lester and Aunt Emma Belle's home. I came down the stairs from my bedroom, curious to see who was at the door because we seldom had company and never that late in the evening. There stood two Nahunta police officers at the door speaking to Uncle Lester and Aunt Emma Belle. As I got closer, I realized that the police were investigating a car accident. I heard one officer offer his condolences for my death. Yes, my death! They all turned in my direction as I approached. "No, Iris was not in any car accident; there she is."

The officers moved towards me and said, "Your father contacted your mother in New Jersey. He told her that you had been killed in a car accident. Your father asked your mother for money for your funeral."

Mom, at that time, was living with her client and boyfriend, John Merlis. He had the good sense to keep her from sending any money until she had contacted the Georgia police to investigate the truth. As someone once said:

"The reports of my death have been highly exaggerated."

I was alive and well!

— CHAPTER 11 —

"ICH LIEBE DICH"

The news that I was not dead but very much alive stirred my mother's heart to want to see me. She had found out where I was living through the police that told her that I was very much alive. That summer, traveling with her longtime friend, Frieda Vanderhorn, on their way to vacation in Hollywood, Florida, she stopped in Waynesville, Georgia, to surprise me.

I was working at Harrison Grocery Store, wrapping pork chops behind the butcher counter at the back of the store, for a customer coming later in the day. I suddenly heard the screen door loudly slam. I looked up and heard a woman's voice in a strong German accent ask, "I'm here to visit Iris. Where is she?" My heart started beating out of my chest as I heard that familiar voice. I knew my mother was in the building. I did not know whether I should run or go to the front of the store. I tiptoed slowly toward Aunt Emma Belle, who was standing behind the front counter at the cash register. I peeked behind a rack, thinking, *Is this real, or am I dreaming? There she stood!*

Mom had shoulder-length flaming red-dyed hair. She was overdressed in a fancy blue satin suit and matching high heels.

My mother was as beautiful as the last time I had seen her when she left us in California. Aunt Emma Belle did not know this strange woman. Mom saw me approaching, and she quickly turned toward me and reached out, grabbed me, and gave me the biggest hug. I was excited but confused about what to do or what to say. I nervously said, "Aunt Emma Belle, this is my mother." We all stood there awkwardly.

Mom asked, "Is there somewhere we can talk?"

"I'm working right now; I can't." I sheepishly looked at Aunt Emma Belle, who answered, "It's fine. You are welcome to go next door to the coffee shop."

As Mom, Frieda, and I entered the coffee shop, customers were staring at Mom in her fancy clothes. There were several booths that were empty. We went to one of the booths close to the window. Mom began talking. I did not hear a word, still amazed that she was really sitting in front of me. Until I heard her say, "Iris, I would like for you to come live with me after we return from our three-week vacation. You do not have to answer me right now. Just think about it, and if you decide you want to live with me, have your things packed when I return." I was shocked.

I loved the people who lived in Waynesville. I was a true southern girl. I did not know if I would like to live in the north, but I longed for a mother. I knew this was my only chance to leave my father's abuse and torment. I made up my mind. I wanted to go. I could hardly wait for her three weeks of vaca-

116

tion to be over. My bags were packed.

After three weeks, I began watching each car that slowed down for the caution light in front of the coffee shop. I was hoping it was my mother's car coming to take me to a better life. It was important that my father not know that I was going to live with my mother. Uncle Lester and Aunt Emma Belle promised not to tell him when he called or came to visit me. I was terrified that he would show up at the same time Mom would arrive. My father's routine was to arrive without any notice to take me for a car ride while he rehearsed his problems or drama with women in his life as if I was his personal counselor. Sometimes I would feel he was trying to make me jealous of the women in his life. I never cared. I just hid my emotions until he brought me back to the store. I went only to satisfy him to avoid his outburst of temper in front of everyone if I refused.

Mom finally arrived to take me back with her. We took our time driving back to New Jersey. We stayed three days in Washington, DC. Our hotel accommodations on Pennsylvania Avenue were at a five-star hotel known for visits from foreign dignitaries. When I opened the window curtains, I could see the city lights of Washington. A politician client of Mom's arranged for us to take a VIP tour of the White House. We had pictures taken at the Washington Monument, the Lincoln Memorial, and many other places. We visited the US Treasury to see how money was made. Believe me, I never had money, and so that was an unbelievable sight.

Mom was embarrassed and somewhat amused that this

backward southern teen did not know what to do with all the silverware and fine china that was presented in the five-star restaurant where we ate food that I could not pronounce. This restaurant was not the southern country diner, better known as the coffee shop, where one could choose a meat and three vegetables at a reasonable price. Just a few days ago, I was putting up canned goods at a country grocery store and cutting meat behind the butcher counter; but now I was living the life of a princess. Mom showed me off to everyone, introducing me as her daughter. She often whispered in my ear, "*Ich Liebe Dich,*" which translated in German was "I love you." At last, I was hearing the words and feeling the love I had not known but desperately longed for.

At night, Mom and Frieda would leave me at the hotel while they had a wild girls' night out on the town, but I did not mind since I was sleeping in the biggest and most beautiful, soft bed with gorgeous linens and a duvet. *If this is a dream, please do not wake me.* As soon as we arrived back at Mom's penthouse in Paterson, New Jersey, she took me shopping for a new wardrobe, including a fancy pink dress, complete with new clothes, shoes, pajamas, purse, and a new hairstyle. She did not want me to look like the southern girl that I was. Two weeks after I arrived, she announced that she had planned a surprise. I was going on a month-long summer visit alone to see my grandparents, Sophia and Hans, my Oma and Opa, in Karlsruhe, Germany. They had not seen me since I left Germany as a baby. I was excited but also scared because I had never flown on a plane. She assured me that the airline would be assisting me on the flight and that there was nothing for me to worry about.

What could happen that I had not already lived and survived?

— CHAPTER 12 —

AMERICAN PRINCESS

I arrived at Frankfurt airport in July of 1963 to visit my loud and proud Opa and Oma. They had a large banner welcoming me to Germany. I was embarrassed by all their fanfare and attention. I was presented with bundles of flowers. They were taking pictures of my every move as we walked through the airport. Opa and Oma could not speak English, but they lived close to the university where a student promised to visit often to interpret for us. Opa drove us to Karlsruhe, Germany, through the beautiful countryside. I could no longer speak or understand German because I had lost the language when I lost my mother. They still lived at 49 Kaiserstrasse, above the cafe and Italian ice cream parlor where I was born. My mother, in her many previous trips to visit her mother and stepfather, had furnished their one-bedroom apartment with nothing but the best. They refused when she suggested that they move to a bigger place. At least to a place that had another bedroom. They told my mother that she did not visit often enough to justify having two bedrooms. On one of her visits, my mother bought them a sleeper sofa for their living room for anyone else who might visit. I slept on their sleeper sofa. They had a clawfoot tub in the kitchen where the pot-bellied stove stood to heat the room and apartment in the winter.

I met my Onkel Willie and Onkel Julius and Tanta Emily and their families while in Germany. Everyone was anxious to spend time with me. They were arguing over who would get to entertain me. Anger is the same in any language. My grandparents were so proud to have their American granddaughter visiting, and everywhere we went, the German people were so warm and friendly. When they heard I was an American, we were given free food and drinks and invited into their homes. We visited Heidelberg and the spa town of Baden Baden, with its healing bath of spring water. We drove into the Black Forest and visited palaces and castles in the surrounding area. I was having a wonderful time being treated like an American princess.

At their apartment one afternoon, I heard a baby crying, and it would not stop crying. "Oma, why is the baby still crying?" I questioned. Oma gestured that she did not understand my question. I pantomimed, holding a baby in my arms, and pulled my fingers down my cheeks to mimic crying. Finally, I saw in her eyes that she understood my question.

Then with a broad smile on her face, she began to swing her hips and laugh. "Katz, Katz!" We both laughed hysterically. I understood what Oma was saying. She was telling me there was a cat in heat in her apartment building. She was laughing, I am sure, because of my ignorance, but I laughed watching her trying to mimic a cat in heat.

A university student came to visit us to interpret anything we needed to understand. Through the interpreter, I asked Oma, "I know my mother wanted to bring you to America. Why did you not come to live with her?"

Oma responded, "Hans never wanted to leave Germany because this is our home. He has his family and friends here. At our age, the change is too difficult. I love Karlsruhe. It is easier for your mom to visit us in Germany." My mother called, and Oma told her about a dinner party we were going to attend at a doctor's home. Oma handed me the phone. I was excited to talk to my mother. "Iris, you are going to a dinner party at a doctor's home tomorrow night. I want you to know that it will be an insult if you do not eat or drink whatever they serve." According to German law, fourteen-year-old minors were able to drink alcoholic beverages. *Why would I want to turn down an alcoholic beverage that I was not going to get in trouble for drinking?*

The next night we arrived at the doctor's home, and the dinner party was as Mom had described. We had a buffet of traditional German cuisine, along with alcoholic drinks and German beer. They had music playing out on the patio. I was dancing with a lot of the younger men. I felt such happiness. I was the life of the party. With all the dancing and beer I drank, I was tipsy when we left the party and returned home.

Opa led me to their bed and motioned for me to sleep with them. I looked at the bed where Oma was drunk and passed out. I was looking forward to getting a good night's sleep on a bed, not the sleeper sofa. I got in the bed and instantly fell into a deep sleep. I was suddenly awakened. I was disoriented as I felt a body pressing into my back. For a moment, I thought it was my father making sexual advances again. I resisted, but he forced me toward himself and continued to caress my body. Terror gripped my heart as the light from the street came through the window, revealing it was my Opa molesting me. He pressed his mouth on mine and began to sexually assault me. When I tried to push him away, he motioned with an angry look for me not to awaken Oma beside me. He finished what he was doing, and I softly cried myself to sleep.

Does pain always follow happiness?

I never looked at or spoke to Opa again during the remainder of my visit. I could not forgive him for what he had done to me. Oma was concerned at the change and sadness she saw in me. She invited the university student over again to the apartment to get to the bottom of what was wrong with me. I lied, telling her I was homesick for home, and Oma easily accepted my answer.

I did not tell anyone about the sexual assault from Opa. After all, who would believe me? Certainly not my mother. She had not believed me when I tried to tell her what had happened at the park when I was almost seven years old. Would she ever believe that I had been sexually abused by a man in the park, then my father, and now my grandfather? Mom would send me away. I began to believe I was responsible for the painful events that kept happening to me. This would be just another scandal that I could not, or would not, share with anyone.

124

I was eager to leave Germany and go home to Mom. Days before I was to fly out, my grandparents were notified there was a problem with my Visa to leave the country. I was anxious about not being able to get away from Opa and return to America. The country did not recognize my United States citizenship. Foreign citizenship laws varied depending on the foreign country. My grandparents had a struggle to finally get permission for me to return to America. It delayed my flight back home for a few stressful days, but finally, I was given permission to board the plane in Frankfurt. At last, I was going to get away from Opa and go home.

"America the beautiful."

CHAPTER 13
WHAT IS YOUR EMERGENCY?

For weeks following my return from Germany, I had flash-backs of the sexual abuse from Opa. My father and grand-father were still in my head and in my bed. I would wake up in a sweat with fear that a man was really in my bed. I would calm myself down by taking deep breaths and repeating the mantra, *I will be okay. I am safe. There is no man in my bed. Opa cannot touch me now.* Then I could finally go back to sleep. My dream of having a loving mother began to turn into *Mommie Dearest.* Mom's lifestyle and the rules she set for me to live by turned the penthouse into a prison, with my mother as the demanding warden. Every morning she would have her usual orange juice and vodka just to get out of bed. Then she would drive me to school in a drunken state. She drank alcohol every day, and her mood would change quickly. I learned to stay away from her to avoid her rage.

When Mom drove me to school, I would plead with her to drop me off a block from the school, hoping no one would see her hungover. She refused, and in defiance, would drive me right to the front of the gate. I opened my car door in embarrassment. Everyone stood and watched her get out of her fancy car to yell goodbye to me. I hurried towards the school door with my head hung low. The high school students recognized what someone looked like after being drunk all night. Mom had no shame anymore, even if I did. Was she trying to numb her pain so she could sleep at night and not dream of the nightmares from her own life? My mother became the person she had been taught by Hitler's Nazi propaganda: *to be indifferent to pain and to have no weakness or tenderness in her.*

It was November 22, 1963. Mom and I were shopping in the Nordstrom Department store for Christmas gifts when over the intercom came the news that President Kennedy had been shot and had died. Everyone gasped with disbelief as people began to cry. Mom was overly distraught over President Kennedy's death. She loved President Kennedy because he was Catholic like herself and had gone to Germany where he said on a visit to West Berlin, "*Ich bin ein Berliner.*" (Translated meaning "I am a Berliner.") She ate and slept very little for days, not leaving the penthouse. We watched television for every report on his death and then the funeral. It was the most compassion and grief I had ever seen displayed by my mother. It was as if President Kennedy was a member of our family.

The mafia expanded Mom's prostitution ring at her apartment. When I came home from school, and the door was locked, then business was in session, and I had to go away and come back later when the door was unlocked. She did not always remember to lock the door. I would walk in on her business and face her rage for the rest of the evening. The beatings became more frequent. I became angrier and more bitter with her and my life. I wore long-sleeved shirts, even when it was hot, to cover the bruises on my body.

I was not allowed to answer the telephone because Mom was also a bookie for the mafia. That's how the bets were made. Sometimes when Mom was gone, just for pure meanness, I would answer the phone acting like I was a dispatcher, saying, "Police station, what is your emergency?" The caller would quickly hang up. It was funny to me, but not to Mom. When my mother found out about my prank, she again beat me and locked me in my room. It was as if she took my father's notes on how to beat someone to hide the evidence. I hated to see men's personal items lined up on the bathroom sink and in the medicine cabinet behind the mirror when they would stay for the weekend. I would often throw their comb, toothbrush, razor, aftershave, and cologne in the apartment hall garbage chute, thinking if I got rid of their things, they would also go away. That never happened. They always came back, the men and their things.

I would stand next to the door where my mother could not see me and listen to her conversations on the phone. Once I overheard her telling someone on the phone that her client had violently beaten one of her girls. She wanted him taken care of and then his body thrown into the Hudson River. When she hung up, I walked into her room and confronted her about her conversation. With an attitude, I said, "Why are you asking someone to throw a body into the Hudson River?" My mother just looked at me with a cold death stare and responded, "Better for you that you forget what you just heard."

Mom insisted that I agree to babysit at the apartments of her call girls that she needed for her clients. Some nights they would not come home all night. I was left in their dirty apartment with their crying babies, listening to the sounds of the street life in a less than desirable area of town. I was too scared to sleep for fear of the drug dealers on the corner and the fighting in the halls. Mom's girls did not live like she did. On nights when my mother had parties in her penthouse, I was always expected to attend. She would instruct me from across the room with her eyes. I learned to read her eyes. I knew what she wanted me to do. Mom eyed a certain man in the room who was one of her wealthy clients that she wanted me to entertain. I would roll my eyes in defiance and ignore her, thinking if I did not look at her, I would not have to do anything. That would only make her furious.

My mother would cross the room and grab my arm, forcing me into another room. Sometimes it was a bedroom, bathroom, or even the kitchen. Then she would beat me with whatever her hand could find—a hairbrush, spatula, pots or pans, anything within her reach. Mom was confident that no one would hear her loud laced profanity and blows to my head or backside. There was loud music playing and conversation drowning out her beatings. Immediately she would push me toward the party, whispering, "You better wipe that smirk off your face and smile, or you will get more from me later." If I did not obey her, I was assured that worse would come after everyone was gone. Why did Mom want me to come live with her? Was she trying to appease her guilt for not being a mother? Was it always her plan to have me in her business?

Mom's boyfriend, John Merlis, was Jewish. He was wealthy and took great care of Mom by paying for her penthouse and her bills. John continued to maintain a home with his wife, Lorraine, and son, Peter. I had seen the pictures of John and Mom's trips to Europe. On winter vacations, they loved to go to Acapulco, Mexico. John always made sure Mom had what she wanted. He was kind to me, but I was not very kind to him. I would glare at him across the table and act as if I did not hear him when he asked me to do something for him. He witnessed how cruel Mom was when she was drunk. John did not object to Mom's life of prostitution if she was always available for him when he wanted her.

John eventually started staying away for longer periods of time, which only made Mom more upset with him. She insisted that John divorce Lorraine and marry her, but John had been honest from the beginning; that was never going to be an option. John had a bad heart, and the stress between Mom and him caused John to worry about their future. He told Mom that he could not divorce his wife because of his religious beliefs. His church would not allow him to be buried at their church cemetery if he was divorced. He also feared he would not have a long life if he continued the stressful life with Mom. John loved

Mom's cooking. She was a gourmet cook, preparing anything, not just German food, but also Italian, French, or Swedish dinners. He especially loved when she would cook Jewish meals. She would prepare for him a Seder meal for two nights of the Passover. She would cook a lamb shank bone, roasted egg, vegetable, two types of bitter herbs, a mixture of apples, wine, nuts, cinnamon, and honey, and she poured four glasses of wine and placed it on the table.

John finally stopped coming to see Mom. He traveled a lot with his work, but now he was not answering her phone calls. She began a frantic search for him. She called everyone that knew John. Finally, someone told Mom he was at the Saint Vincent Hospital in New York (closed on April 10, 2010). She insisted that I go with her to visit John at the hospital. Traffic was bumper-to-bumper and moving extremely slow, nothing new for New York City traffic in the middle of the day. Mom decided to park her car. She stood out on the road and flagged down a taxi. The taxi driver drove us to the entrance of the hospital. The elevator door opened on the third floor. We went to the front desk, and Mom asked the nurse, "I would like to visit John Merlis. What is his room number?"

The nurse looked up and asked, "Are you family?"

Mom quickly answered boldly, "Yes, we are John's family." I gave Mom a disapproving look. The nurse directed us to John's room.

John was in a coronary care unit (CCU), a specialized intensive care unit for heart patients, where John's heart function was being monitored closely. John was asleep as we walked into his room. The room was dimly lit. I was hoping John's wife would not show up unexpectedly while we were there. Lorraine knew Mom. They both hated each other. Mom called out to John, "Please, John, wake up. It's Ida, and I'm here, darling."

John slowly opened his eyes and whispered, "Ida, how did you find me?"

Mom sweetly whispered, "I knew something had to be wrong; you were not answering my calls." John glanced over at me and threw his hand up to acknowledge me but did not say a word directly to me. I took a seat in the corner of the room while Mom stood by his bedside. Mom took his hand and questioned, "Why did you not have someone contact me? I would have come to be with you."

John first turned his eyes toward the window and then slowly turned his eyes back to Mom and sternly demanded, "Ida, I did not want you to come. We cannot go on like this. My heart can no longer take the stress with you and your life. I have decided I am going back to Lorraine and Peter. You must not come here again. Please just leave before she comes walking in the door." I could tell John was getting weaker as he spoke.

Mom began crying and leaned over and lovingly stroked his hair while tears ran down her face. She responded, "John, I have always loved you, and this cannot be the end. You're only talking like this because you're so sick. You will get better, and

133

when you get out of the hospital, I will bring you home with me." John began whispering again, and Mom leaned closer so she could hear what he was saying. I could not make out everything, but the few words I heard, John was telling Mom it was over between them and for us to leave.

Before Mom could say another word to John, the nurse came running into the room and sternly demanded, "Mr. Merlis needs to get his rest. You must leave." The nurse probably thought Mom was crying because of John's condition. Mom was crying because she knew she would never see him again. She hailed a taxi for us to return to her car. Mom was quiet as she drove us home. John never left the hospital; he died two weeks later. Mom did not attend his funeral and never spoke of him again.

John had faithfully practiced his symbolic religious rituals while living his adulterous life.

— CHAPTER 14 —
GOOD TIMES ARE HERE

Mom handled John's death by denial. She ignored her heartache. We stayed at a five-star hotel in New York while Mom filled our days with shopping at the best shops on Fifth Avenue. We dined at Mama Mia Restaurant, her favorite Italian restaurant, where we were treated like celebrities. Money gave her influence and respect, even when it was earned through disreputable means. We went to Radio City Music Hall to see shows. We even went to see their famous annual Christmas Show with the Rockettes.

Mom loved Yorkville's Germantown on the upper east side of New York. Music was always important in Germantown. Mama would loudly sing her songs, raising her beer stein in the air, dancing the polka, remembering her homeland. No matter how much she drank and danced, she was unable to handle John's death. Mom and I walked with our friends from Germantown in the annual Thanksgiving Day Parade, presented by Macy's. The three-hour event is still held in New York City. We were dressed in the traditional German Dirndl dresses with frilly blouses and a tightly fitted bodice. We waved to the crowd like movie stars. Everyone was standing along the streets, applauding us as we passed by. Everyone must have thought our lives were great. No one knew what life was really like with *Mommie Dearest*. There were floats, professional bands, and live animals borrowed from the Central Park Zoo. At the end of the parade, Santa Claus was welcomed into Herald Square.

We occasionally visited Saint Patrick's Cathedral Church, which was a neo-Gothic church located on the east side of Fifth Avenue between 50th and 51st Street in midtown Manhattan. I never forgot the beauty of the cathedral. I was awestruck whenever I entered the cathedral with Mom. I sat on the pew, staring up at the tall ornate ceilings while she lit candles. Each lit candle represented her own personal faith and prayers. The lighting of the candle was a particular form of supplication and was a way to remember loved ones or to pray for special needs. I recalled visiting the cathedral for the first time when I was six years old. Years later, after I knew the truth, I wondered if the memory of the Catholic priest who sexually assaulted her tortured her soul while Mom stood in the cathedral. She stayed a long time in the confessional booths. After returning home, she would act kinder, but it never lasted. She would return to her fits of rage in her drunken stupor.

I began to realize that if I was going to survive, I needed to manipulate Mom's guilt to my own advantage. After a beating, I would get her to buy me anything I wanted. My love had turned to hate, so I got some revenge by manipulating her guilt. I missed John because Mom was kinder when he stayed in our home. He would defend me when she went into a rage over something I had done or said. There was no pleasing Mom. I would spend most of my time with my friends from school. She did not care what time I came home, as long as I did not interrupt her lifestyle. I was determined that:

I would survive!

— CHAPTER 15 —

MOMMIE DEAREST

I wrote letters to my best friend, Elaine, in Waynesville, Georgia, about *Mommie Dearest*. While I was at school, Mom found one of my letters that I had not mailed yet to Elaine. When I came home from school and stepped off the elevator, I saw two suitcases by our front door. I was excited because that meant Mom would be out of town on one of her client trips. I immediately smiled, thinking of the fun Patricia and I would have while Mom was gone. I hurried into our apartment. I could not wait to hear where she was going and when she would leave. As I entered the penthouse, Mom was seated in a chair, shaking papers in her hand, rocking back and forth with her head down. She looked up at me with a scary glare. "Are you leaving on a trip?" I asked. "When and where are you going?"

Mama stood up, shaking the papers in my face, and said furiously, "You are the one leaving."

"Where am I going?" I questioned. My heart was beating so fast, and my hands were shaking.

"You are going back to Waynesville or anywhere else you

decide. I really don't care. You are just getting out of my home."

"No, please don't kick me out!" I pleaded.

Mom yelled, "I read your letter to Elaine. How dare you tell those things about our private lives to other people?"

"I'm sorry, I will not do it again. I didn't mail it. I'll tear it up. Mom, I promise I didn't mean those things I wrote. I was just mad with you at the time. Please give me another chance."

"You're not going to defy me again. I will not tolerate you any longer. You are not happy here, so go back to Waynesville, Georgia and see if that will make you happy," she demanded.

"Please, please don't do this. I will do better, I promise. Mom, please, just let me stay," I pleaded.

Her mind was made up, and I was not changing it. She was furious that I had exposed our life to someone else. She demanded that I bring my two packed suitcases as she headed for the elevator. Mom drove me to the train station to send me back. There was a deafening silence in the car as we rode to the train station. I could hear her heavy breathing as I stared out the car window, knowing that I would never see her or this place again. I was filled with so many conflicting emotions. I wanted a mother, but not this mother. This was the death of my dream of a happy home life. The rejection I felt from my mother was intolerable. I started thinking of my future plans.

I'll call Elaine. She'll come and get me at the train station. I can make it without Mom. Then the fear overwhelmed me again. *What am I going to do?* I refused to allow Mom to see how upset and frightened I was in the back seat. I denied the tears that were filling my eyes, forcing my emotions not to reveal themselves. We arrived at the train station. There were only a few people on the platform. Mom went to buy my ticket; then she walked over to me and, without any emotion, said, "Here is your ticket and money. You can call someone to pick you up." Her last words to me were, "I know that you'll go back down south where you will stay poor, barefoot, and pregnant." She turned away, not saying another word. I watched her drive away without ever looking back.

I heard that lonesome whistle blow.

CHAPTER 16

FOOL'S HILL

I ran to a payphone on the platform and quickly called Elaine before the train arrived and explained to her what had happened. "Mom found a letter I had written to you and kicked me out," I relayed.

"Just because of a letter? What was in the letter?" Elaine questioned.

"More of the same about my life with *Mommie Dearest*," I responded.

"I cannot believe she would do that," Elaine replied.

"Well, believe it. I'm on my way back to Waynesville. Elaine, will you ask someone to bring you to the train station to get me?"

"Yes, of course. What time will your train arrive?" Elaine asked. I was crying so hard I had a hard time getting out the words.

"Noon tomorrow. Could I stay with you for a few days until I figure out what I'm going to do?" She agreed. I cried so much during the sixteen-hour trip that I had no more tears when I got off the train at Nahunta, Georgia. Elaine was waiting for me.

When she spotted me in the crowd, Elaine began to run toward me and embraced me, saying, "I am so sorry your mother has done this to you."

"I will be all right. I did not want to live with her anyway." I answered boldly. We headed for her home in Waynesville, Georgia, where I stayed for a few days.

After I left her house, I slept wherever I could find a bed. Every home that I slept in was not a safe place. One night at one of the homes, I came out of the hall bathroom dressed for bed. My friend's father was coming down the hall at the same time, so I stopped to say good night when he grabbed me, pushed me up against the wall, and sexually assaulted me. There are three survival instincts that we develop. It is either Fight, Flight, or Freeze. I chose to freeze with fear, hoping that my best friend or his wife would not come out of their bedroom. I knew I would again be blamed for the encounter. I finally came to my senses and threatened to scream, so he quickly turned and went to his bedroom.

The next morning, I made up an excuse that I appreciated their kindness, but I needed to move on. I could not bring myself to tell anyone the truth because I did not want to cause anguish for them, lose a friendship that I treasured, or I would have to leave Waynesville because no one would believe me. He was well respected. I did not have any other place to go. I just stayed wherever I could, from one place to another.

Elaine was not the only person I talked about my life with *Mommie Dearest*. I was dating Don Gibson. I began sharing some details with Don about my life after moving to New Jersey to live with Mom. While I was living in New Jersey, after Mom would go to bed, Don and I would talk on the phone until wee hours of the morning about *Mommie Dearest*. Although he did not know all the skeletons in my closet, he knew enough.

Don had enlisted in the United States Marines. He was deployed to a military base in California. When Don heard that I was back in Waynesville, he asked a friend to persuade me to call him. When Don answered my call, I hesitated, then mumbled, "Hi Don, I heard you wanted to speak with me."

Don replied, "I have been told you have nowhere to live. Please let me help you."

"I do not need your help. I have places I can stay." I lied. He knew I was lying and that I had no place to live. I was living basically on the street. Don had already contacted his parents, Pete, and Marion, pleading my case for them to allow me to move into their home until he returned from his deployment.

"Iris, you are welcome to live at my parent's home until I return."

"Your parents are not going to let me live with them," I argued.

Don promised, "They both have agreed, and you can move in today."

I reluctantly accepted his offer and moved in with my two

suitcases in hand. They had a nice home with a guest bedroom and bath, located at the side of the house by the garage, for me to live in. Don's mother, Marion, had a problem with stuttering when she spoke. From the beginning of my stay, she was very cruel. She always glared with disapproving eyes and clearly did not want me staying in her home. Don and his dad, Pete, must have convinced her to allow me to stay. I ignored her disapproving attitude to keep the peace. Pete was very kind and compassionate about all that I had been through. Pete was upset with how Marion was treating me. He wanted me to be happy living with them. Marion walked around as if there was a dark cloud hanging over her head. I tried to avoid her because I needed a place to stay. Don was excited that I was waiting for him in his home until he returned.

My father had heard I was back in Waynesville, and he started his routine of calling and harassing me. I could not figure out how he would always find me. Wherever I moved, he would locate my address and phone number. The phones in those days were called a party line. My memory was of picking up the telephone, which was a party line, and listening to the conversations of strangers. The party line rescued me many times when my father would not hang up. Someone would pick up the phone and ask to use it. That made him furious. He would end his conversation, like a broken record, repeating, "You are a loser and will never amount to anything. Even your mother did not want you." His phone calls always ended in us fighting. Even though he could no longer hurt me physically, his disapproving angry words still hurt. Children often quote, "Sticks and stones may break my bones, but words will never hurt me"—what a lie! Broken bones can heal, but words can affect your life forever. It breaks down your mental well-being day after day. It's a mental injury that is difficult to heal. Others will say it's a mental illness, but to me, it means more than just an illness; it's a *mental injury. It can affect the rest of your life.*

One afternoon while home alone, I received another phone call from my father. I knew he had been drinking again, with his thick-tongued voice, slurring his words. I could have hung up on him but always feared he would show up at their door, and that would only make things worse. After my father hung up, I was seated on the living room sofa, sobbing. I was so depressed and feeling overwhelmed with my situation. *When will my father's torment of me ever end?*

Pete came in early from work and saw how upset I was. He came over and sat next to me on the couch. Trying to console me, he put his arm around me while I sobbed on his shoulder. I was telling him about the phone call from my father. "I will put a stop to your father's phone calls and stop him from tormenting you anymore." Pete kindly promised.

In defeat, I whispered, "You will not be able to stop him. My father will never leave me alone. You do not know what he is capable of doing."

Suddenly, without warning, the door opened, and in walked Marion with her arms full of grocery bags. She glared at us sitting on the couch with Pete's arm still around my shoulder. She dropped her bags on the coffee table. She assumed the worst and went into a screaming rage, stuttering as she yelled, "Y-y-you, l-l-little tramp! How d-d-dare you, g-g-go after m-m-m-my husband? G-g-get out of m-m-my house. Get out!" and she meant now. I could not answer. I just ran back to my room by the garage. I paced back and forth around the bedroom, my heart beating so fast I was convinced I was going to have a heart attack. I could not think. *Where will I go? What will I do? I have no money. How can I take care of myself? I just want to die.* I thought I really loved Don and was waiting for his return by staying in his parents' home. I eventually realized I did not love Don as much as I *needed* Don. I just hated my life, and I thought he was my way of escaping the emotional abuse and the pain of loneliness.

As I was pacing and packing, I recalled a librarian named Mary Lou Gibson who had befriended me at Nahunta High School. She was married to Pete's brother, Fred Gibson. Numerous times while I was at school, Mrs. Gibson allowed me to come to the library and talk to her about anything. When I had a rough day, she always knew and would sign an excuse to get me out of my class and stay in the library, helping her on some project. I called Mrs. Gibson on the phone and on the very last ring she answered. I nervously apologized. "Mrs. Gibson, I am so sorry to call you so late, but I need help. Would you please come and get me from Pete and Marion's house and let me stay with you just tonight?"

Mrs. Gibson replied without asking why, "Of course, I will be right there. Just watch for me outside by their mailbox."

"Thank you so much, Mrs. Gibson; I will explain more when I see you."

She drove over immediately, even though it was late in the evening. I was standing outside by their mailbox with my two suitcases in hand when she arrived. I put my suitcases in the back of her car, and we left without speaking to Pete or Marion. We traveled down Browntown Road, on that pitch-dark dusty, dirt road, headed for her home as I rehearsed the events of the evening. "I'm so sorry that Marion acted and talked to you in that manner. She was wrong for kicking you out of their home. Honey, everyone goes over Fool's Hill at least once. Marion has run over that hill more than once." Mrs. Gibson reached over and patted my hand and smiled. "Do not cry anymore. You can stay with us tonight. We will figure it out in the morning."

Out of the darkness will come the dawn of a new day.

— CHAPTER 17 —
TON OF BRICKS

The next morning at the kitchen table, Mrs. Gibson set my breakfast in front of me and said, "Iris, Fred and I talked it over last night, and we would like for you to live with us. We'll help you graduate next year."

I started crying. "You do not have room for me. I have nothing to give you in return."

"You do not have to pay to stay. We'll make room for you," she kindly responded. This kind, generous, God-fearing couple asked me to call them Mom and Dad Gibson. They had two daughters, Freddy Lou, nineteen years old, Sarah Anne, sixteen years old, and a son, Tom, ten years old. They were loving, very simple, and modest people who shared what little they had with me. They could not afford the three children they already had, much less take on another mouth to feed, but they never hesitated to take me in.

Now there were six of us living in a modest two-bedroom, one bathroom, wood-frame house, which setback from highway 84. We, three girls, slept in one bed made from two twin beds pushed together in the back of the house where there was no heat. Mom Gibson's handmade quilts were piled on top of us to keep us warm in the winter. When we woke up in the mornings, Freddye Lou, Sarah Anne, and I would try to outrun each other across the screen porch to be the first one in front of the pot-bellied stove in the kitchen. It gave us the only heat in the house. After we were warm enough, we dressed for school. Tom was the youngest, and he slept in Mom and Dad Gibson's bedroom.

After my traumatic exit from Don's parents' home, Don quit calling from California. It really did not matter anymore. I would never want to be part of his family. Mom and Dad Gibson helped me graduate from Nahunta High School in June of 1965. Neither of my parents came to my graduation. Dad Gibson co-signed a note for my first car, a white 1960 Ford Falcon. After graduation, I moved from Waynesville to Brunswick, Georgia. I rented a house with my friend, Naomi. It had two bedrooms and one bath. I thought I had finally escaped from my parents now that I was on my own. Surely, they would leave me alone, but they always found me. I could not escape their verbal abuse.

My father was having treatment at the Veterans Mental Health Hospital in Savannah, Georgia. His psychiatrist called me. He commented in a hurry, "I believe your visits would assist in your father's mental health recovery. Also, your father wants to speak with you concerning his financial matters."

I responded, "I will see what I can do. Thank you for calling."

I did not want to visit my father. His doctor did not know my truth, and I was not going to tell him. My father had several mental breakdowns, which put him in and out of veterans' mental facilities. He was haunted by a theory that the military had planted a microchip somewhere in his body while he was serving overseas in Korea. He believed that the government was spying on him because he had threatened to expose unlawful acts and atrocities that he saw, approved by the army, during the Korean War. None of which he could prove, and I am sure were a fabrication in his mind. I was puzzled why my father wanted to talk about his financial matters when, as far as I knew, he never had any money. It was a long, almost two-hour drive to the hospital. I sat in the hospital parking lot for another twenty minutes before getting the nerve to go inside. I signed a book at the front desk, and they pointed out where I should go to find my father.

My heart was beating as loudly as the sound of my heels on the tile floor. I slowly walked down the hall to a door with a small window. I nervously peeked in the window and saw my father seated at a table by himself. He was in a ward with mental patients who were clearly delusional. The door creaked when I slowly opened it, but no one looked my way. I approached and stood next to him. He did not look up when I spoke. I sat down across from him. He looked up then stood up to hug me, but I pulled away. "Okay, I'm here. What do you want to tell me?"

A male nurse interrupted us to give my father his medicine.

I watched the black male nurse show kindness and attention to a man who had always shown racial hatred but was now accepting this black man's kind hand of care. He sat all alone with no friends or family to come and visit. I slightly smiled with some satisfaction, knowing he could not harm me in this place. The only friendly face he saw day after day was a black male nurse. My father was racist. How ironic that he was in a state of acceptance from a man who was treating him better than he deserved.

I asked my father again impatiently, "Answer me, why did you want me to come? What financial matters did you want to discuss?"

He responded, "Being here has proven to me that there's nothing wrong with me. I do not belong here with all these crazies. I am not a lunatic. The only problem I have is my drinking. If you promise to come to visit me after I get out, I'll stop my drinking, but you must promise to come to visit me." He always had an angle, so he did not have to admit he was an alcoholic. He refused to give up his drinking for anyone else before and surely not for me. I would not enable his addiction anymore.

"When you return to Brunswick, I'll come to see you," I promised because it was what he wanted to hear. I wanted to leave him and all the craziness that I was witnessing in the room.

As I drove almost two hours back home, I was filled with intense disgust that I had been compelled to visit him. *Why did he want me to drive so far just to tell me that he would stop his drinking if I started to visit him? After all, he could have told me that on the phone. No daughter should see her father in a mental ward.* Then it hit me like a ton of bricks. He had won again. He was testing me to see if he still had control over me by making me visit. It was more about my coming at his beck and call than what he said to me. I had no desire to see him again, but I doubted he would ever leave me alone.

I felt desperate, and I did not want to live like I was living anymore. I thought the only way out of my deepest darkest pain was to commit suicide. I made my plans to drive my car off the road, hit a tree, and die instantly. I was driving to work when I realized this was my moment to end my life of pain. I quickly jerked the steering wheel of the car, driving off the shoulder of the road into a wooded area where my car hit a large hole, which stopped me just a few feet from a huge tree that probably would have killed me. I damaged my car and got a bump on my head and bruised my shoulder. I could not even commit suicide correctly.

After telling my best friend, Naomi, about my suicide attempt, she scheduled an appointment with a doctor for me to get help. Dr. Thompson admitted me to the hospital for depression and a nervous breakdown along with having seizures at the age of seventeen. I was having epileptic seizures that would recur with vigorous shaking. The seizures occurred suddenly, without warning, then I would lose consciousness. After consciousness returned, I would have a severe headache and extreme exhaustion.

I was kept on medication to cope with my depression and

seizures. I was released from the hospital with an unlimited number of tranquilizers and seizure medication. If I really wanted to die, the doctor had just given me my way to do it. As I left the hospital, I heard an inner voice, "You will live and not die."

I did not want to die; I just wanted to end the pain of living.

— CHAPTER 18 —
CRUISE OF A LIFETIME

After I returned home from the hospital, I did not want to leave the house. I felt like I had no hope. No purpose. No plan for my future. Naomi knew I needed to get out of our house and start living again. On weekends, she insisted that we go cruising in my 1960 white Ford Falcon to meet new friends at the Twin Oaks Drive-In Restaurant in Brunswick, Georgia. Young people met there on weekends to hang out, visiting from car to car. Twin Oaks Restaurant was famous for their best hamburgers and hand-cut, floured french fries. The waitresses took your order car side while wearing skates.

It was an unusually chilly Saturday night for the month of September in 1965. Naomi insisted in a determined voice that we needed some fun and we were going to Twin Oaks. I reluctantly agreed. As I drove around circling Twin Oaks, I saw a good-looking man with his arms crossed, leaning against his 1957 red and white Ford Fairlane with another man. He caught me staring at him and smiled. I quickly looked away, saying, "Naomi, that guy by that Ford is cute. Let's drive around again and take another look. Oh, he even has a friend for you!"

Naomi spotted a car pulling out of a parking spot next to them and excitedly said, "Iris, hurry and back your car into that spot so we can get them to come over and talk to us." The waitress skated over and took our orders. We both kept smiling towards the two guys who knew we were flirting. They finally slowly walked over to my car.

The first guy, the good-looking one I had admired, with his dark black hair, must have been six feet tall. He leaned into my open window and said, "Hi there, do you believe in love at first sight—or should I walk by again?"

I blushed and nervously laughed, not knowing what to say. I was attracted to him and his dreamy hazel eyes. "You are too funny; what is your name?" I asked.

He quickly responded, "My name is Chris Wainright. What's yours?"

I played shy, looking down while I answered, "I'm Iris Arnett."

Chris responded, "Where are you from? I've never seen you here before. Somebody better call God because He's missing an angel."

Naomi was busy talking to Chris' friend on the other side of the car. When she heard Chris' comment, she stopped and looked towards me, laughing. "Wow, he's a keeper, Iris!" I gave a thumbs-up under the seat as I turned back to Chris and said, "I was living in Waynesville, but after we graduated from Nahunta High School, Naomi and I moved here." Trying to change the subject, I responded, "What is your friend's name, talking to Naomi?"

"He's Larry Bennett. We've known each other for years. He camps out on our couch when he needs a place to spend the night."

We began laughing when Chris told me where he was living. It was across the street from where Naomi and I were renting a house. We spent the next couple of hours laughing and flirting the night away. Before we left, Chris and I exchanged phone numbers. We started talking on the phone until late every night, sharing everything—well, almost everything. I could not let him know all about my dirty little secrets, or he would reject me too. Chris gave me my reason to live. Over the weeks, Chris told me that he drove an ambulance for Edo Miller Funeral Home. When he was on call, he would spend his nights sleeping upstairs at the funeral home. In those days, ambulances operated out of the funeral homes. When a call came in, the ambulance was dispatched to the emergency, assisting and transporting a person to the hospital. Chris enjoyed driving the ambulance and helping people with medical emergencies.

Chris was so much fun, and I desperately needed fun in my life. I would often come out to get in my car, and on the windshield, there would be a poem or something funny that he had written and left for me. I had low self-esteem and did not love myself or feel worthy of being loved. I wondered if I was capable of being loved. He told me after a couple of months of dating that the first time he had seen me cruise through Twin Oaks

Restaurant, he leaned over to Larry and said, "There goes the girl I am going to marry."

One morning I washed my hair, put it up in large rollers, and wrapped a scarf over my head, which was a common practice among young women at that time. I was out of coffee for breakfast, so I ran out the door to drive to a nearby grocery store with my large hair rollers on my head, still wrapped in a scarf. On my way, I saw Chris in my rearview mirror driving behind me, motioning for me to pull over. My heart raced with excitement as I got out of my car to get into his car. As we were talking, he drove off with me without a word about where we were going. He suddenly turned down a narrow alleyway, stopping at an unfamiliar house. He left me in the car as he went inside, saying, "I'll be right back." A few minutes later, he rounded the corner with an older woman. "Mother, I want you to meet the girl I've been telling you about." As I got out of the car, I was mortified and thought, *Oh no, I look like a Martian from outer space!* "Mother, this is Iris. Iris, this is my mother, Eva Lou Welch."

My face flushed as I extended my shaky hand and said, "It's so nice to meet you." I saw a hint of a smile across her face. We stood there and talked for several uncomfortable minutes of awkward conversation. No one seemed to know what to say.

Finally, Chris broke the silence and said, "Mom, we need to get going. I've got to get Iris back to her car; it's parked on the side of the road. I will not be home for supper." She nodded, turned, and went back into her home.

160

I was embarrassed to meet his mother for the first time with a wet head, and all decked out in large rollers. I was annoyed with Chris forcing me to meet his mother before I was looking my best. I got out of his car and slammed the door, letting him know that I was not happy. I shouted, "You can go to supper by yourself." Later, as I reflected on this incident, I realized that this was a man who could love me despite how I looked.

I did not really know anything about loving someone else. I maintained a survival mode. My plan was just trying to get through the day, not thinking about long-term plans. It was all about my next twenty-four hours. My goal was to avoid having a tragic day. I would just hang on from one drama to another. I was always on the brink of failure, which became my normal, but who could sustain that kind of life? I started working in downtown Brunswick at Highsmith Jewelers on Main Street. Chris continued to work with his father at W. & T. Tile Company. I was getting more serious about Chris and began thinking about our future. I was not sure of Chris' future because he seemed to keep everything to himself. He was always funny but seldom serious.

One Saturday night, we were parked at our usual place in the woods. Chris shared how he never knew his biological father, who had left his mother after his birth. His stepfather, Rudy, became the only Dad he had ever known. Rudy was working in Brunswick, Georgia, and owned the W. & T. Tile Company. Chris was five years old and his sister, Glinda, was seven when Rudy and Eva Lou met each other. They fell in love and eventually married. Rudy had several tile projects he had to finish in Toledo, Ohio, after they married, and he wanted his mom to go with him. Eva Lou left Chris and Glinda in the care of her mother, Billie Pagonis, while she left for Toledo. Rudy and Eva Lou reunited with Chris and Glinda when they moved back to Brunswick, Georgia, about three years later. It touched my heart that he was sharing more about his family.

Chris quickly changed the subject, grabbed my hand, and said, "Let's get out of the car and sit on the front hood of my car. I promise we will be able to see the stars through the trees." We both laid back on his car's windshield, listening to the car radio blaring, staring at the sky, when I saw a shooting star.

I shouted, "Look at the shooting star. Quick, we must make a wish."

Chris said with a twinkle in his eye, "I have something better than that." He lifted me off the hood of his car. He passionately embraced me in his arms. "Iris, remember what I told Larry the first time I saw you drive through Twin Oaks?"

"Oh, you mean that I was the girl you were going to marry. That was funny, huh?" Chris got quiet and looked away as in deep thought. I nervously said, "I'm sorry, that is probably not what you were remembering?"

"Iris, I love you with all of my heart, and I cannot think of my life without you. I want to marry you and have you as my wife and the mother of my children. Would you marry me?" Chris knelt on one knee and presented an engagement ring to me. I was so shocked; this was so unexpected because we had only been dating five months. I did love being loved by Chris.

I squealed with excitement, "Yes, of course, I want to be your wife and the mother of your children." I laughed with joy. Chris slid the engagement ring on my finger. I rambled on about how beautiful my ring was. I then had a thought, *Do his parents approve?* I cautiously asked, "Do your parents know you are asking me to marry you?"

Chris laughed. "I told them earlier today. They approve and are very happy for us. Now I better get you home; it's late, and you have to work in the morning."

I went to work the next day at Highsmith Jewelers, flashing my engagement ring to the other employees, and of course, it dominated every conversation I had with potential customers. The owner did not share my joy when he overheard his customer ask where my fiancé, Chris, had purchased it. I immediately named another jewelry store down the street. I was fired before my shift ended. It did not take long after I was fired to realize I would not be able to pull off the wedding extravaganza I was planning. It would be more than I could afford. We moved the date and planned for a smaller wedding. Some of my friends suspected that I must be pregnant to hurry and get married. I could not have been pregnant because Chris refused to have sex with me until after we were married.

I made an appointment to have my physical exam, which was the custom, to get a marriage license. I arrived for my appointment early in the morning, so I could still make my afternoon shift at my new job at Kentucky Fried Chicken. After the doctor's examination and blood work, the nurse directed me into the doctor's office to wait. After a while, I decided the nurse must have forgotten about me waiting to see the doctor. I had to get to work. I was not waiting any longer. As I reached for the door handle, the doctor quickly entered the room. Doctor Thompson, with a look of concern, said, "Iris, where are you going? Please have a seat. I apologize. I had an emergency which took longer than I had planned." As he rounded his desk, he blurted out, "Iris, are you and your fiancé planning on having children?"

I had been seeing Doctor Thompson for several years, and he knew some of my background. "Of course, we want children. My dream is to have two girls and two boys," I proudly responded.

"I am sorry to inform you, but you will not be able to carry any children. It would be too dangerous for you." He extended his hand across his desk. "I want you to stay on these birth control pills. Schedule an appointment in a month. We will discuss how you are doing on the pills when you come back." Stunned, I left the building sobbing, broken-hearted. Having children was my dream. I desperately wanted to be a mother. I called into work where I had only been working for less than two weeks. I lied and told them I was too sick to work my shift.

How am I going to tell Chris I can never give him children? That he will never be a daddy? I will never be a mother!

That night, Chris arrived for us to go out to dinner. He noticed I was being very quiet. He asked me, "Are you all right? You're not saying much. Have I done something wrong?"

"I'm fine." I was so distraught; I could not talk about how I was truly feeling while we were in public.

After dinner, as we stopped in front of my apartment, I reached over to open the car door as Chris reached over and stopped me. He put his arm around me and said, "Come on, Iris, now tell me what is bothering you."

I quickly snapped, "I do not want to marry you. I need more time to figure out my life before I jump into marrying someone I hardly know. We have not been dating long enough to really know each other. This is all going too fast for me."

Chris lovingly said, "Iris, look at me! What has brought this on? You have been excited about us getting married. Are these wedding plans too much for you? Let's just elope and not go through all this. I love you, and we will get married."

I blurted out, "I cannot have children! I will never be able to give you any sons or daughters."

"Of course, we can have children," Chris promised.

I replied, "No, Doctor Thompson told me this morning that I will never be able to carry any babies."

Chris responded, "Did you ask Doctor Thompson why you cannot have children?"

"I was so shocked and upset. I just wanted out of there. No,

I didn't ask. The doctor told me I could not carry babies; what does it matter why?"

"I don't care if we ever have children; I still want to marry you! I love you, and we will be getting married. We can always adopt if you want to have children," Chris promised.

I laid my head upon his shoulder and cried. I was both happy and sad. I did love Chris, but once again, the cycle of failure made me feel ashamed. This time it was because I could not have children. What if he knew my hidden profound disgrace? Would he still want to marry me? I was damaged goods.

We decided to have our wedding at Faith Chapel on Jekyll Island, Georgia, because Chris' sister, Glinda, had married Ray Thomas at Faith Chapel on July 18, 1963. It was a beautiful, small chapel. It would be perfect for the limited number of guests we were inviting.

I longed to have someone seated on the empty bride's side of the church. I was like any girl who would expect and want her mother at her wedding. I called Mom. I was so nervous that I could hear my racing heart beating loudly. She answered on the first ring. "Hi, Mom, are you busy? I need to talk to you about something very important."

"I have some errands I need to run, but it can wait for a few minutes. I have not heard from you in quite a while. What is so important?" she asked.

I was so excited as I rehearsed the events of Chris proposing to me and how beautiful the engagement ring was. I proudly replied, "I love Chris, and I am happy. Chris' family approves of us getting married."

Mom said in a disapproving tone, "I do not know anything about this Chris. Who is he? How long have you been dating this guy? What does he do for a living? Where do you plan to live?"

"Mom, I know things have not always been good between us, but I would love to start over so you can get to know Chris. We have been dating for five months, and Chris is the best thing that has ever come into my life. He works for his father, who owns his own business, W. & T. Tile Company. His mother helps his father with accounting. We already have an apartment that I have moved into."

Mom raised her voice as she responded, "Five months! That is all the time you've known this man. Why are you rushing into marriage? Are you pregnant?"

"Mom, I am not pregnant! We love each other, and we want to be together. Please just come to our wedding. Please, will you come, and maybe Frieda would come with you?"

"Iris, I do not know if I will be available. I'm very busy right now. What is the date?"

"We have almost a month before we get married. It will be March 25, which is a Friday, at 8 that night."

"I will see what I can do. If I can make all the arrangements to fly, I will try and work it out to come. Let me talk it over with Frieda and see what her schedule looks like and let you know."

"Thank you! Mom, I do hope you will come. It would mean a lot to both of us." She hung up abruptly without saying goodbye.

I was so excited that she might come and witness Chris proclaiming his love for me and my love for him. I could not sleep; I just kept seeing my mother seated on the front bench of the church pew as I walked down the aisle to my handsome groom. Despite all my feelings of anger, hatred, and unforgiveness toward my mother, I was still hoping that if she was at our wedding, we could start a new chapter in our lives. We had not seen each other since Mom put me on a train sending me back to Waynesville years before. Over the years, there have been many dramatic phone calls between us. There were too many terrible memories, and it was time for us to have some happy memories.

Prior to our wedding, Chris had found an apartment for us. Each apartment had one bedroom and a half bath in a building with other tenants. There was a shared bathroom in the hall of the building that had the only tub and shower. The apartment building was located across from the Brunswick Court House. I moved what furniture I had and clothes into the apartment. Chris' plan was to live with his parents until after our wedding. He was a man of integrity and very proud. He did not care what others thought of him, but he did care deeply about damaging my reputation by living with me before we were married. Mom arrived at the airport with her best friend, Frieda Vanderhoven, two days before our wedding. I was planning on sleeping on the couch and gave my bedroom to Mom and Frieda. I was excited to show Mom our apartment and our wedding gifts from several wedding showers Chris' family had given us. Mom's face revealed it all. "You could not expect Frieda and me to share a hallway bathroom with strangers?" Mom arrogantly proclaimed. "Take us to the nearest hotel. We will not be staying here."

Stunned, I replied, "I know this is not what you want for me, but I told you that I love Chris, and I can be happy living anywhere as long as we're together." I turned and walked out of the room as I recalled the last place Chris wanted us to rent. It had cracks in the bedroom ceiling. I jokingly said to Chris, "You can see the sky during the day or stars at night just by looking up."

He laughed and said, "It would be romantic to lay in bed and see the stars." We both laughed as we simultaneously said, "What will happen when it rains?"

That night during the rehearsal dinner, I nervously introduced Mom and Frieda to Chris, Rudy, Eva Lou, and their family. Mom politely greeted them but displayed her condescending attitude throughout the entire evening. I felt the humiliation of Mom's behavior. She drank more than she ate, which made me more anxious as the evening progressed. I never knew when she might go into a rage over any little thing that displeased her. This play was one that I had seen too many times. The next day, I met Mom and Frieda at the hotel for breakfast. Mom was already drinking as usual, as we discussed the plans for the day and what time they should arrive at the church. Frieda tried to get Mom to lower her voice and calm down, but without much success. Mom bitterly asked, "Last night at the rehearsal dinner, you did not include me as the one who would walk you down the aisle. I should be walking you down the aisle to give you away, not Mr. Gibson. I am your mother. How dare you deny me this honor?"

I repeated, "*Dad Gibson* will be walking me down the aisle. That's not open for discussion."

She replied, "He's not even family. I'm the only family you have at your wedding."

"To me, Dad Gibson and his family are my family! I was living from house to house. They welcomed me into their home when I had nowhere to live." I stood my ground.

Frieda reached over and grabbed Mom's arm as she sternly said, "Now, Ida, this is Iris' wedding day. Enough! We need to leave to get her wedding veil. Iris needs to get back to their apartment to get ready for her wedding. Come on, Ida, there is much for us to do before tonight."

We left the restaurant to get my wedding veil in silence. As I pulled up to our apartment, I quickly said, "Let me take my veil upstairs, and I will be right back to take you to your hotel." Mom got out of my car and quickly walked toward me. I turned, and I saw her piercing, angry stare. I thought she did not hear what I had said. I repeated it once again, "Mom, I will not be long. I am just taking my veil upstairs, and I will be right back to take you and Frieda to your hotel." She never said a word; her eyes said it all; she suddenly drew her hand back and slapped me across the face so hard it caused me to fall and drop my veil in the dirt. I stood up with my veil in my hands and brushed the dirt off as best as I could. I was determined not to let her see me cry. Nothing had changed between us. I was sorry I had invited her to come to our wedding. I could not remember a holiday or special occasion; there was not any drama from Mama. I whispered as I turned to walk away, "I will call a taxi for you to go back to your hotel." I quickly ran upstairs and made the call. I looked out the window, watching them standing at the curb until the taxi arrived and took them away.

I turned eighteen years old on February 22, 1966. Our wedding took place at Faith Chapel on Jekyll Island on March 25, 1966, at 8 p.m. The description of this monumental event in my life was written in the *Brantley Enterprise* on the front page of the newspaper, along with three funerals, one birth, an article on Boy Scouts, a parent-daughter Future Homemakers Banquet, and an article on Questions and Answers on the Bible. A reporter had published our wedding as the news for the week. There was my picture in the newspaper along with an article about our wedding. "The bride wore a white gown of Peau de Soie with a scooped neckline, fitted bodice, and long sleeves with wide cuffs of Chantilly lace. The slightly flared skirt featured long back pleated panels forming a train. A three-tiered, shoulder-length veil of French illusion was attached to a crown of simulated orange blossoms accented with seed pearls. She carried a cascade bouquet of white roses, stephanotis, and ivy."

171

Freddie Lou was my maid of honor, and Jimmy Hudson served as Chris' best man. Reverend Eugene Reese of Waynesville Baptist Church performed the ceremony, and Marshall Allen performed the music. I was so happy and proud that something good was finally recorded in my life. At the rehearsal dinner, Chris reminded me, "Honey, keep your eyes on me, and everything will be all right." I began walking down the aisle on the arm of Dad Gibson; I did not look at Mom. I learned not to look at Mom's eyes for her approval, disapproval, or correction. I kept my eyes straight ahead to my soon-to-be-husband.

As I approached Chris, he had tears in his eyes. I saw in his eyes the love, joy, and excitement that he was feeling. I felt the power and emotion of the moment, also, and my heart was full of love for Chris. My eyes filled with tears too. The ceremony was everything I had dreamed of. Pastor Reese told Chris, "You may now kiss your bride." Everyone started clapping. We walked down the aisle as Mr. & Mrs. Chris Wainright.

After the wedding ceremony, the photographer took pictures of us by the altar and in front of the church. He had to ask Mom several times to stand closer to me so he could take the family bridal picture. I was determined nothing was going to take away the joy of my wedding day. Our reception was held at Chris' parents, Rudy, and Eva Lou Welch's home, on Union Street in Brunswick, Georgia. Mom began telling unflattering stories about me to my new in-laws. They must have been worried about their new daughter-in-law.

Chris and I gave each other a bracelet engraved with the

words that Chris had previously written in a love letter to me: "More Than Yesterday, Less Than Tomorrow."

Would our love be more than it was yesterday— but much less than it would be tomorrow?

PART 3: THE REST OF THE STORY

KINGDOM OF DARKNESS OR KINGDOM OF LIGHT

To ignore there's spiritual warfare happening is naive—*I know, I've done it.* There is a real adversary out there who wants you depressed, anxious, and suicidal. We don't need to be preoccupied with the enemy, but we do need to be aware of his schemes so that we can stand against him. There are going to be times when it seems darkness is creeping in. In those times, pull out God's Word and begin to take authority over the powers of darkness by turning on the light.[1]

For the longest time, I was totally in darkness, but I know now that *God has rescued me from darkness and transferred me to the kingdom of His Son* (Colossians 1:13).

---

6. Leslie Stephens

175

— CHAPTER 1 —
EVERYBODY LOVES LOVE!

We spent our first honeymoon night at the Wanderer Hotel on Jekyll Island, Georgia. It was a nice hotel, except that the walls were so thin that we could hear the couple in the room next door who were not quiet about what they were doing. "If we can hear them, Chris, they can hear us." I blushed.

"Well, honey, let's give them something to hear!" I blushed even more!

What does love mean? Could it be the first time you wake up and hear the one you have just married softly breathing next to you? For that moment, you do not feel fear, loneliness, shame, or rejection. What a feeling, this must be love. We had promised in our wedding vows to love, comfort, honor, and keep each other for better or worse, for richer or poorer, in sickness and in health, and forsaking all others, be faithful only to each other so long as we both shall live. I was determined not to follow in my father's footsteps, who married ten times. Our love, I believed, was strong enough to stand till death do us part!

The next morning, we ordered breakfast sent to our room,

and then we left for Florida for our weekend honeymoon. We stayed at a hotel on the beach. We went swimming in their indoor heated pool. We were not shy about our passion at the shallow end of the pool when we realized an older couple were walking towards us. It was obvious that it had been a long time since their honeymoon. He was white-headed, and she had dyed black hair with grey roots. They were carrying a cooler with towels over their arms and were walking toward a table and chairs near us. They gave us a disapproving look as they passed us, and we overheard him saying, "Get a room!" We giggled as they walked off; clearly, they decided not to join us in the pool. I had never felt this happy, and I was loving it.

On our way back from Florida, we stopped at Six Gun Territory, where we watched a gunfight and walked the dusty trails of a western town from a time long past, arm in arm; we could not take our eyes off each other. We stopped at one of the little town stores and had a newspaper printed with the headlines—"Chris & Iris, Honeymoon at Six Gun Territory." Chris, the jokester, had me laughing all the time. We were talking about everything, everything, except my past hidden life. We were on our very best behavior. We had eyes only for one another. Other people would smile as if they knew we must be honeymooners. *Everybody loves love.* Nothing Chris or I wanted to do really mattered if we were doing it together. We were wrapped up in each other's happiness. We just loved everything about each other. Life was so good! This was a new feeling, a new positive attitude for me.

After the weekend, we returned to our one-bedroom apartment across from the Court House. I returned to work at Kentucky Fried Chicken while Chris continued his job as a tile setter with his father at W. & T. Tile Company. I had cooked for my father and brother, but I was not a good cook. Mom was a fabulous cook but did not have the patience to teach me. I was not allowed in her kitchen unless it was to clean up after the meal. I could not make those fancy meals she insisted we have for her guests.

I had heard Chris say he loved fried shrimp. I wanted our first home-cooked meal to be special. I had bought a pound of fresh shrimp from shrimp boats along the East River at Oglethorpe Bay at the downtown Brunswick docks. I thought by the time I got off work, at 5 p.m., it would take too long to prepare the shrimp. During my lunch break, I went home to clean, peel and boil the shrimp to save time when I got home later to fry them. Yes, I was going to fry the boiled shrimp. Chris' surprise supper was ready for him when he came home from work. I cleaned the apartment and put up some of our wedding gifts that were waiting for us when we returned from our honeymoon. I kept running to the window to watch for him to drive up and park in front of our building. When I saw him drive up, my heart started beating so fast, my face even flushed with excitement. I had never cooked a meal for Chris. We had been eating out every meal. I was thrilled to have him home to eat our first meal in our first apartment. I even had music softly playing in the background.

I ran to meet Chris at the door with my hair and makeup

flawless. I had changed clothes twice so that he would like what I was wearing. I opened the door before he had a chance to turn the knob. "Hi, honey, I'm so glad you are home. Tonight, I have made your favorite meal. Please wash your hands; supper is ready." The table was set with lit candles in the middle. Everything was perfect.

Chris replied, "Let me take a shower and change my clothes. I am so filthy from the tile work we did today."

"I do not care; you are just fine the way you are. You do not have to change for me, and besides, I do not want supper to get cold." That statement would be tested. He washed his hands and came to the table where everything was ready for him.

He asked, "How did you know that I love fried shrimp?"

"Honey, of course, I know; I have listened to everything you have said about what you like and do not like. It is important to me for you to be happy. I want to be a great wife."

I watched him take his first bite of shrimp, and he just chewed and chewed and chewed. "Is there something wrong with the shrimp?"

"No, honey, it's great. I really appreciate you cooking tonight. I have gotten tired of eating out every night." Chris replied. It was terrible, but Chris ate it all. It was not until the next day at work I found out what I had done.

"Martha, you are a great cook. What did I do wrong when I made fried shrimp for supper last night?"

Martha questioned me, "How did you prepare it? Because it is very simple to fry."

"Well, I ran home yesterday during my lunch break to boil the shrimp so it would save me time when I got home. I fried the boiled shrimp before Chris came home."

Everyone was laughing, "Girl, you don't boil shrimp before you fry it. It must have tasted like rubber!"

"Yes, it did taste terrible, but Chris never uttered a word. He ate every bite."

Martha laughed and said, "You guys must still be on your honeymoon!" I had a lot to learn about being a wife. It made for a good laugh for a good while. Love is so kind.

The next week Chris answered the phone. "Oh, hi, Dad. What's up?" I knew by his expression that it was bad news.

I interrupted Chris several times, "What is wrong? Answer me! What is going on?"

Chris whispered, "I will tell you in a minute." Finally, Chris hung up and turned towards me with a shocked look on his face. "Dad's friend is on the army draft board and saw my name on the draft list. Men are being drafted into the army. If I do not want to be in the army, I have to enlist in another military branch of my choice before the army draft comes knocking."

Uncle Sam wants you!

— CHAPTER 2 —
ANCHOR'S AWAY

We were married a month when Chris enlisted in the United States Navy. He had never gone anywhere outside of Brunswick, Georgia, except on a class trip to Atlanta, Georgia. He promised, "Sweetheart, after we are married, I am going to take you to see the world." Now he was leaving for the world without me. Chris and his friend, Earl, enlisted in the US Navy under the buddy system so they could be stationed together. They were sworn in on May 2, 1966, in Jacksonville, Florida, before leaving for boot camp for ten weeks. Chris was sent to Chicago, Illinois; Earl was sent to San Diego, California. They never saw each other again. So much for the buddy system that the navy promised when they enlisted.

I moved into my in-laws, Rudy and Eva Lou Welch's home, while Chris went to boot camp. Their home on Union Street had large cedar trees lined on each side of the sidewalk, ushering guests to the steps of the rocking chair front porch. It was an older two-story modest southern style home with three square columns on the porch. The home featured four bedrooms and two baths. The owner's bedroom and bath were on the main floor, and the other three bedrooms and bath were on the second floor. I shared the second floor with Chris' grandmother, Billie Pagonis, who lived in their home.

Rudy operated his W. & T. Tile Company from the warehouse behind their home. Grandma worked at a laundromat, washing and folding clothes for customers who would drop off their laundry earlier in the day. Everyone loved Grandma. Chris told me stories of himself as a young boy, taking naps under the table while Grandma folded clothes for her customers. He spent his afternoons going to matinees at the theatre close by. Surely, I had found happiness now that I was part of this loving and happy family.

I finally received Chris' pre-typed form letter from boot camp, which came two weeks after his departure. It gave me his address and short Do's and Don'ts for me to follow in contacting him while he was at boot camp. Chris returned home from boot camp on July 15, 1966, but only for two weeks before he left for Millington, Tennessee, where he would attend Aircraft Mechanic School. Five months later, at Christmas, Chris returned to me at his parent's home. His military orders were to leave in January of 1967 to a training squadron at Whiting Field in Milton, Florida. We decided that I would stay at his parent's home until he was settled before I would follow. A week without his bride was enough for Chris. He left camp, drove all night, to bring me back to Milton, Florida; what Chris did for love.

I washed clothes for Chris' navy buddies to make extra money. At night, we partied with friends, drinking and dancing at local bars. We picked up bottles on the side of the road to return to the store for pennies. Those pennies added up enough to get us a pack of cigarettes.

I had lost contact with my brother, Mark, who enlisted in the army. He was only eighteen years old and was sent to serve in Korea on the DMZ, while Chris' orders moved us to Norfolk, Virginia, on January 15, 1968, to serve in an aircraft squadron, which was detached to the *USS Yorktown CVS-10*.

The nights were becoming difficult again unless I had been drinking too much before I went to bed. The flashbacks had returned. I was having vivid nightmares again. Chris would snuggle me during the night, and when it awakened me, I was terrified, thinking it was my father or grandfather. I would react by pushing him away. I was overcome with remorse when I realized it was my husband. When Chris tenderly asked, "Why are you pushing me away when I reach for you?"

I quickly apologized, "I'm sorry; I just got too hot lying next to you. I'm just hot-natured." He seemed to accept my excuse. I was still protecting the hideous lie. The traumatic reason for shame could not be exposed. I believed that Chris would be shocked and reject me.

I was feeling so tired and sick all the time. Convinced it was the flu, I made an appointment to get a physical. I went to see the navy doctor on base, and after his examination, the doctor shocked me with his announcement. I was pregnant. I had been on birth control pills since we married. I never expected that I would be able to get pregnant just because I may have missed taking pills once or twice.

To celebrate, I rushed to get a cake from the nearest bakery. I was thrilled and could not wait for Chris to get home. I met him at his car. "Honey, hurry up inside; I have to show you something in the kitchen." We rushed through the door and into the kitchen, and he looked at the cake on the center of the table with the words, "We are having a baby!"

"Are you kidding me? We are having a baby?"

"Yes, we are having a baby. I'm so excited I cannot wait."

Chris reached out and hugged me as he beamed with joy, "I'm excited, too, but you must be very careful." We were over the moon with excitement but concerned that I may not be able to carry full term. Dr. Thompson had told me I would not be able to have children. I quit partying, drinking, and smoking. I had a reason to be on my best behavior.

I was nineteen years old when our daughter, Laurie Lynn, was born at a civilian hospital, the Santa Rosa Hospital, in Milton, Florida, on July 8, 1967. She was so beautiful with her wisp of blond hair and blue eyes. She weighed seven pounds, eleven ounces, and was twenty-one inches long. I was so in love with my newborn daughter. She was healthy and perfect, definitely of more value than the $25 we had to pay for the $5 a day medical bill. Chris was paid $32.50 every two weeks while he was detached from the ship *USS Yorktown* and was always paid in cash. I received a check from the navy for $92 a month for living expenses.

I knew nothing about how to take care of a baby. I read all the books I could find on how to be a good parent. I was so happy. I was convinced that Laurie would keep me happy. I was committed to her never being abused. My life's purpose was now very clear.

I must be the mother my mother never was!

— CHAPTER 3 —
IT FEELS LIKE HOME

As time passed, Chris and I stopped talking or listening to each other. He was gone most of the time, serving on the *USS Yorktown* or on tours of duty. Otherwise, he worked part-time as a mechanic at a local Sunoco Gas Station. Chris gave his time and energy to the United States Navy or his navy buddies and had very little left for Laurie or me. My thoughts became negative, and I became critical of my husband, and it showed in my actions. My feelings began to change. In the past, I had been abused by men; therefore, I was determined not to be rejected or controlled by any man. Chris had been raised mainly by women—mother, grandmother, and his older sister, so he refused to let another woman tell him what to do. We each had our own heavy baggage that we had brought into our marriage.

We were both self-absorbed, not caring about each other's happiness. We had forgotten our wedding vows. Every day my attention was on my daughter's happiness, not on my husband. I no longer met him at the door when he returned home from work. I didn't care if I pleased him with how I was dressed. Many times, when he came home, I still had a worn, tattered

189

robe on. I had convinced myself Chris was coming home late anyway; I could not see a reason to make the effort. I no longer saw love, only disappointment in his eyes.

Laurie was a little over a year old when we found out I was pregnant again. Chris wanted more children, so he was excited about another baby on the way. I was worried because my last pregnancy was difficult, and I was afraid about being able to carry another baby full term. Mom and I had not seen each other since our wedding. The phone rang, I answered, and to my surprise, it was Mom in a good mood. She asked, "Why don't you and Laurie come to visit me in New York City for a weekend trip, all expenses paid?"

"Let me talk it over with Chris and let you know." It was not difficult to convince him to let us go since we both needed some time away from each other. I was excited that Mom would be able to have time with her first grandchild.

I was very naive and believed that our relationship would be better between us since I was bringing her granddaughter to visit. What grandmother does not love her first grandchild? After all, Mom was the one who invited us to come and visit. She had to have changed her attitude towards me. I had made it very clear on several phone calls that it was Mom's choice if she wanted to be part of our lives. We flew from Norfolk International Airport into LaGuardia Airport, where Mom was waiting with a bouquet of flowers, jumping up and down with excitement and waving a big sign welcoming us to New York. We arrived early in the morning, so we had all day to visit with

Mom. Things started out great. She had planned four busy days with shows, great restaurants, shopping, and visits from her friends. Mom only had a couple of cocktails at lunch and was on her best behavior. We went to the afternoon show and then made a quick run through Macy's to shop. I was exhausted when we finally arrived back at her penthouse. An hour later, her friends arrived so Mom could proudly show off her daughter and granddaughter over dessert, coffee, and her many cocktails.

By the next morning, when I saw her make her third vodka and orange juice for breakfast, I knew trouble was ahead. We rushed out the door to get in a full day of sightseeing. I would have been happy to stay at her penthouse where Laurie could play and I could rest; after all, I was pregnant. Mom had plans, and I had to do what she wanted to keep the peace. Mom had everything orchestrated down to the last minute. Laurie, being two years old and out of her routine, was very moody, clingy, and crying a lot, which was wearing on Mom's nerves.

At lunch, Mom had more alcohol to drink than food to eat, which made her loud and boisterous in the crowded restaurant. She was rude to the server, and she was loudly complaining about how I was not taking care of my daughter. I did not want a scene, so I kept quiet, not making eye contact, hoping we could get out of the restaurant without more of a scene than she had already created. We went to FAO Schwarz to shop for toys for Laurie and our baby on the way. I made an excuse so I could call Chris from a payphone while Mom told the salesman where to mail our packages. I explained to Chris the events that I was watching as the old pattern of behavior was unfolding. She had been verbally abusive at the restaurant, so now she was buying gifts to appease her bad behavior. Chris insisted, "What is your problem? You can handle your mother another twenty-four hours, then get on a plane and come back home."

That night Mom was drunk and had become very abusive again as she screamed about everything; she felt I was doing wrong. "You do not know how to take care of a child, and you're going to have another one? You do not even feed Laurie the right food. I do not know how she is still living."

The penthouse was not big enough to stay away from her. As I stood in front of her pleading, "Mom, please go to bed. I'm too tired. I need to go to bed. Your loud voice will wake Laurie. Please, let's talk in the morning." I tried to walk by her to get to the bedroom, but Mom reared back and slapped me across the face so hard it knocked me against the wall. Before I could say anything, she turned, walked over to her telephone, and called for a taxi to take us to the airport. Mom screamed, "Now, get out of here and do not ever come back!"

I packed our suitcase and left it by the door. Without speaking to Mom, I picked up my sleeping daughter and carried her to the elevator, going down to wait for the taxi. I sent the taxi driver up to her apartment to get my luggage. On our way to LaGuardia Airport, the taxi driver crashed into the side of another taxi. The crash threw us around in the backseat, but with no serious damage. I was an emotional wreck. Laurie was not the only one crying. The taxi drivers did not even call the police; they just screamed out the window at each other in a language I did not understand.

When we arrived at the terminal, the taxi driver told me that Mom had already paid for the trip and tip when he went to her door for my luggage. Yes, I was none too surprised because that was her method of operation. We waited for hours at the airport for a seat on the next flight back to Norfolk, Virginia.

Why does the victim keep going back to the abuser?
It's because it feels just like home.

The term "trauma bonding" was coined by Patrick Carnes, who developed the term to describe how the "misuse of fear, excitement, and sexual feelings" can be used to trap or entangle another person. Put more simply: trauma bonds occur when we go through periods of intense love and excitement with a person, followed by periods of abuse, neglect, and mistreatment. The cycle of being devalued and then rewarded over and over works overtime to create a strong chemical and hormonal bond between a victim and his or her abuser. Therefore, victims of abuse often describe feeling more deeply bonded to their abuser than they do to people who consistently treat them well.

Anyone who is in an abusive relationship can become trauma bonded to their abuser, but people who experienced traumatic relationships as children may be more prone to these types of bonds. After all, we already experienced these types of relationships with our parents or other caregivers, so our nervous system is already primed up to fall into the cycle.

193

Signs of trauma bonding:

1. You want to leave someone, but you simply cannot bring yourself to cut them out of your life;

2. You're in a relationship that you would never want any of your loved ones to be in;

3. The person has some characteristics that remind you of a toxic parent or another caregiver;

4. You find yourself trying to get back to the past. (You've lost your grasp on reality); and

5. You're justifying behavior that you know is wrong.

From my own research, I studied "trauma bonding" relationships. I learned that after the abuse, the victim's brain memory of the abuse is not based on reality. The victim takes the blame for any abuse. Recovery occurs when we come out of denial. We honor what we are feeling, what we know and what we sense to be true. We recover our God-given ability to be wise and trust the changes we know need to take place to bring health and healing back into the relationship if that is possible. I know that very well from my own life. You can research for more information on "trauma bonding" or "how the brain works against the abuse victim" to fully understand the consequences and recovery. Trauma can have a lasting effect on your mental, physical, and emotional health struggles.

After I returned home from the traumatized visit in New York with my mother, I made an appointment with a navy doctor to assure myself there had been no harm to my pregnancy. After my examination, the doctor was concerned about my pregnancy. Since I did not have anyone except Chris in Norfolk, Virginia, the doctor wrote a letter to Chris' commanding officer, requesting that he would be exempt from the upcoming three-month Mediterranean tour of duty aboard the *USS Yorktown* to support me. Before dawn, we watched the *USS Yorktown* leave the port from our car window as Chris rushed me, in labor, to the Portsmouth Naval Hospital in Portsmouth, Virginia.

I was twenty-one years old when Angela Michelle was born at 5:20 a.m. on September 2, 1969. She weighed seven pounds and was nineteen and a half inches long. She had some curly blond hair and big blue eyes. She looked like a beautiful porcelain doll. My doll baby was healthy, and that is all that mattered. I went home from the hospital after five days. We got even more good news: there was no medical bill for her since she was born at the navy hospital.

I vowed: my daughters will never know abuse!

— CHAPTER 4 —
CYCLE OF ABUSE

Chris received his honorable discharge from the navy in January 1970. We moved from Norfolk, Virginia, back home to Brunswick, Georgia, to live close to Chris' family. Brunswick is a resort city on the southeastern coast of Georgia on a harbor near the Atlantic Ocean. It is bordered on the east by the Atlantic Intracoastal Waterway, which separates it from the Golden Isles. It is the second-largest city on Georgia's coast. With a deep-water port, Brunswick has thriving seafood and shipping industries. It was on those docks that I had bought the fresh shrimp for our first supper. Even with the Brunswick Golden Isles Airport, there were no career opportunities for Chris as an aircraft mechanic. He did not go back to work with his father in the tile business. Instead, he accepted a job with the Brunswick Hercules Plant, a gum and wood chemical manufacturing company, as a boilermaker, fabricating structural steel. He also worked part-time as an auto mechanic at a BP gas station.

Even though I had two beautiful daughters and an honest, hardworking husband, I was unhappy with my life. I believed a husband was supposed to make his wife happy. I expected him to fulfill all my needs, and in my opinion, he was not even trying. We were just going through the motions of being married. He had his family and their love. I did not feel accepted into their family. Of course, it was all in my mind; they tried to make me feel welcome. Chris shut me out of his life by keeping everything to himself. I was very lonely and felt abandoned. He would go into his "man cave" and not come out when I was upset. He thought if he ignored my behavior, it would soon pass. Our home had too many loveless moments. When growth stops, decay begins.

Chris was a very content person. I was a jealous person and resented my husband's attention toward anyone other than me. Chris had little ambition. I had too much ambition. He was the one that slowed down for a caution light; I was the one who would speed up. He hated confrontation. I liked confrontation. He liked keeping everything on a steady course like a ship. I was always ready to rock the boat. Chris was forced to walk around on eggshells, so I would not get offended. He never knew what would cause me to lose control and become abusive, especially with how I spoke to him. My hatred of men was being taken out on my husband. He could do nothing to please me. I would belittle him in front of other people. It all really demonstrated how badly I felt about myself. I ran back into my dark hole of self-pity.

The voice of shame was loud and clear, again reminding me of my past. I was testing his love for me, believing surely his love would fail and he would leave me, so I thought, *Let's get on with it. I will give you a reason to leave!* Guilt says I've done something wrong, but shame says there is something wrong with me. I still hid my guilt and shame from Chris. I was back in the same city where my father still lived. He had heard that he was a grandfather. One afternoon while I was gone to the grocery store, Chris answered the phone and, to his surprise, the man told him that he was my father. I had never told the truth to Chris about my father. Chris promised him that he would give me the message to call him back so we could arrange for him to visit his granddaughters as soon as possible.

When I got home, Chris said, "Honey, your father called today and wants to come over to see his granddaughters. Why have you not told me about your father? You acted as if he was dead, but now I find out he is very much alive. You did not let him know about his granddaughters?"

"I do not want to talk about him. He is not going to come here to see Laurie and Angela. That is all you need to know." I was not going to allow my father into my daughters' lives. Chris could not understand my reaction towards my father. I refused to return my father's calls. I did try in the past to talk to Chris about my father, but I could not speak the whole truth; I was too ashamed of my past. This created another wall in our marriage for me to hide behind; instead of Chris offering support for me, it further alienated our relationship.

I constantly needed Chris' approval and demonstrations of love to be happy. I no longer cared if he was happy. I wanted to be happy. I was in a *cycle of abuse*. I was now the one that was abusing others with my tongue. I was just as abusive to the sales lady at a department store or the cashier at the grocery store as I was to my husband. The problem was no one knew how to help me. They just ignored me, hoping that I would change on my own. That is like telling someone bound by addiction to just stop their addiction. I hated what I was doing as much as everyone else did.

We rented a house across the street from Chris' sister, Glinda, her husband, Ray, and their three sons, David, Kevin, and Randy. She always wanted a daughter; she loved when the girls would come to visit. I was jealous of their love for her. I lived in torment of losing my daughters and my husband. I did love Chris, and I needed to hang on for dear life. One night I had too much alcohol to drink, which was becoming routine. We were fighting about Chris' sister, Glinda, keeping Laurie and Angela at her home. I was jealous of my girls wanting to be with Glinda more than me. Glinda was a very loving, patient, caring, wonderful wife and mother. I never felt like I measured up to her high standard. Glinda did not deserve my attitude and behavior.

I would scream and slam cabinets and doors to get Chris' attention. He would only walk out of the room without saying a word. Every time there was a crisis, I felt alone to deal with it. Chris would resort to our bedroom to escape the drama. He refused to fight with me, and it's hard to fight when you're the *only one in the ring*. I could not admit that I had a drinking problem, but after being drunk one night, I awoke early the next morning

200

without Chris lying next to me. I stared at the ceiling, trying to remember anything about the night before. Even worse, I could not remember where my girls were. I jumped out of bed and tearfully searched the house but could not find anyone. Chris was gone. Laurie was two years old, and Angela was six months old, and they were gone too.

I was in a panic, crying, running around the house screaming. "Laurie, come to Mommy." Suddenly the door opened, and in walked Chris with Angela in his arms, holding Laurie's hand. Laurie ran to me, putting her arms around my legs. I took Angela from Chris' arms and held her tight as I wept about the kind of person I had become. He had taken the girls to spend the night with Glinda when I started fighting the night before in a drunken stupor. The thing I hated about my mother was her drinking. I vowed I would never be like her.

I had become my mother.

— Chapter 5 —
Only God!

Our daughter, Angela, was only eleven months old when she became very ill. For days she was vomiting, diarrhea, crying all the time, with a high fever. I called Chris at work to let him know I was on my way to the doctor's office. Seatbelts did not become mandatory until 1985. I placed Laurie on the backseat and held Angela against me as I drove fast across the causeway from Brunswick over the bridge to Saint Simons Island. After her checkup, the doctor informed me, "Angela's fever is still 105, and her vital signs are serious. You need to take her to Brunswick Hospital. I have already called ahead, and the doctor is expecting you."

I was trembling with fear as I called Chris at work. When he answered, I said in a panic, "Meet me in the emergency room at the hospital. Angela is critical."

Would I lose my daughter as I had always feared? Chris was waiting at the entrance to the Glynn Brunswick Memorial Hospital emergency room when we arrived. He took Laurie as they immediately hurried Angela to the doctor who was waiting for her. They suspected that she had spinal meningitis. A spinal tap was done, which came back negative. Angela was in the pediatric ward with five specialized doctors assigned to her medical case. Her symptoms did not reveal her illness nor give them a diagnosis.

She was in the intensive care unit across from the nurses' station. Our baby was laid in an oxygen tent to give humidified oxygen, strapped to IVs administering medicines, which were not working to make her better. I could not hold her. She was too little to communicate her symptoms. Angela's vital signs were deteriorating moment by moment. By this time, I had been at the hospital with Angela for over a week while Glinda kept Laurie. Chris continued to work at our Car Care Centers that we owned. He was only a few minutes from the hospital. He tried to be with us as much as possible and still manage our two businesses.

We stood in the hall while the doctor told us to prepare that Angela would probably not make it through the night. I went back into Angela's room, but I could not bear watching my sweet baby, lying weak and drugged into sleep with IVs from her nearly lifeless body. I could not breathe with such anguish. I had to get out of her room, if only for a few minutes. I left Chris sitting by Angela's bedside. I started walking down the long hall of the hospital. I was emotional with my heart broken. The doctors could not save our baby. I desperately needed someone to save our baby. People had stopped me all week as I walked down that same hall. They asked if I was the mother of the baby who was so sick. They would try to encourage me;

they were praying for me and Angela. We were on their church's prayer chain. Where were they now? I was enraged at God. I wanted someone to stop me again in the hall so I could scream at them, "Your prayers did not work! There is no God! My baby is going to die."

I suddenly stopped walking, wondering where I was going. I could not run away. I must be at Angela's bedside. God must be punishing me for being a bad person and being a failure as a mother and a wife. I looked up and saw a sign on the door in front of me that read "chapel." I opened the door, peeked inside, and, seeing no one, I quietly walked in. I slowly moved toward the front to an altar. Stained glass windows were across the back of the small room, and there were a few padded pews.

I began crying again and screamed, "Is there a God? Do You even care that You're taking my baby? You have taken everything from me. If You are a real God, give me back my baby, and I promise I will serve You the rest of my life." I laid my head down on the pew in front of me and cried till I could not cry anymore. Then I stood up, walked out of the chapel, and returned to Angela's room. The doctor had ordered me a sedative to calm me down. The nurse insisted that I go to bed in the empty room next door and get some sleep. I refused to leave Angela's bedside, but I did insist that Chris go home and get some sleep. I promised to call him when he needed to return for the worst. Our home was minutes from the hospital. Chris was getting very little sleep himself. He stayed with me some nights, allowing me to get some sleep. Then during the day, he was operating our businesses. He was constantly keeping the family and friends updated on Angela. Chris was heartsick, too, and felt powerless to save his baby girl.

I finally agreed to take the sedative to calm my nerves, and it was not long before I was unable to sit up. The nurse escorted me to a vacant room next door to Angela's room to get some rest. She promised she would wake me when necessary. I immediately drifted off to sleep from the sedative. About 3 in the morning, I was awakened by the nurse who was shaking me, saying, "Hurry, your baby is sitting up, and she is crying for you." I jumped up and ran into her room, where she was sitting up in the oxygen tent, which she had not done for days. She was reaching out for me, crying, "Mama."

The nurse put her arm around me and said, "Honey, I believe she is going to be all right." I lifted my head with tears streaming down my face and shouted:

"There is a God!

— Chapter 6 —

Just as I Am

The doctors were astonished by her recovery. It was a divine miracle that we took Angela home two days later. The following Sunday, I went alone to Southside Baptist Church to fulfill my promise to God. Several people welcomed me as I entered the foyer of the church. I found a seat about halfway down the aisle. The congregation sang songs from a Baptist hymnal. When Pastor Tex Woods began preaching, my heart was pounding so loudly I wondered if the people seated next to me could hear it. Tears were streaming down my face; I could not stop crying. I, for once, did not care what others thought about my crying.

I was anxious for Pastor Woods to finish preaching so I could get up and walk down the aisle. I believed that church was the only place to find God. I did not know you could pray anywhere, anytime, to accept the living God. When the pastor finished his sermon, they started singing, "Just as I am." I was the first to jump up and walk down the aisle. I stopped at the altar with my face in my hands while tears kept flowing down my face. Pastor Woods stepped down from the pulpit to greet me. I looked up at him and nervously whispered, "Would you teach me about this God who has just given my baby back to me?" The pastor repeated my words to the congregation.

Pastor Woods turned to me and asked, "What is your name?"

"My name is Iris Wainright."

"Iris, would you like to ask Jesus into your heart and be saved?"

I answered, "Yes, because I promised God I would serve Him if He saved my baby. All I know is God did give Angela back to us."

The Pastor continued to explain what it meant to be saved. That I had to admit that I was a sinner, he read out loud from Romans 3:23 (KJV), "For all have sinned and come short of the glory of God." Well, duh, I knew that pretty well. I had rehearsed that fact most of my life. I was a sinner. I was hoping he was not about to ask me what those sins were because that probably would have killed the deal. I did not think that I was good enough to be loved or accepted by God. I knew I was a failure. I believed I would never amount to anything. Pastor Woods responded in confidence, "God loves you." John 3:16 (KJV) reads, "For God so loved the world that He gave His only begotten Son, that whosoever believes in Him should not perish but have everlasting life."

He told me there is power in the cross where Jesus Christ had died for my sins; that the blood of Jesus Christ has the power to cleanse me of all my sins once and for all. I repeated the sinner's prayer after him. "I confess with my mouth that Jesus is my Lord and do believe in my heart that God has raised Jesus from the dead. I accept that I am saved."

He read from Romans 10:10 (NIV). "For it is with your heart that you believe and are justified, and it is with your mouth that you confess and are saved."

That means I would be forgiven for my past. He advised me to read and study the Bible, so I would learn more about who God is. Pastor Woods reached over and hugged me, saying, "Welcome to the family of God." No man other than Chris had ever hugged me without it making me feel dirty, defiled, and ashamed. I felt like someone had just lifted a heavy weight off my heart. I felt peace flood my soul. I felt *loved*! I did not feel alone or afraid. I had a feeling of joy and peace that was truly unspeakable! The Holy Spirit had awakened and stirred in me a hunger and passion for knowing the person of Jesus Christ.

I looked forward to going to church with Laurie and Angela every time the door opened. Chris did not like how much time I was spending at the church. I invited him, but he did not want any of that "religious stuff," as he called it. Chris asked, "Is the pastor good-looking?" as if that was the reason I was going to church so much.

I just laughed and replied, "Come with us and see for yourself."

My desires changed. I no longer wanted to drink. Boy, I

loved to drink alcohol and swear like my mother. I did not have to make myself give up anything. I just had a change of heart. My heart wanted to read and study God's word from the Bible and get to know this Man, Jesus Christ, who gave His life for me when I was just a sinner and not deserving of His forgiveness and grace. I was not a person who liked reading books. I have a learning disability, dyslexia, whereby a person fails to attain language skills of reading, writing, and spelling. It is caused by an impairment in the brain's ability to translate images received from the eyes or ears into understandable language. Suddenly I was reading the Bible for hours a day. I became so heavenly-minded; I was no earthly good.

My mother had walked into new territory, America, and did not understand the language or the customs.

I was now walking into new territory, the Kingdom of God, where I did not understand the language or the customs.

Faith, not fear. Forgiveness, not resentment or revenge. Joy, not depression. Love, not hate. Truth, not lies. Tithing, not getting money but giving it away. Peace, not chaos or trauma.

I had much to learn about this new kingdom.

— CHAPTER 7 —

BUMMER LAMB

I called Mom on the phone, convinced that I had all the answers. I could tell her what she needed for her life. I wanted her to know that I had accepted Jesus Christ. In my naive way, I tried to tell her about how she needed God. I was so excited because she could find the peace that I was feeling. I did not know about her past life story at that time. Her belief was *the church was a place of betrayal and not a place she could find refuge.* She was furious that I had joined the church. "Iris, I am so upset with you. You are so stupid to believe this religious garbage fed to you by the lies of a pastor. Do not speak to me again about church or God." "But, Mom, God gave Angela back to me. She almost died, and God healed her."

She did not want to hear about a God she believed had taken her baby. She slammed the phone down, refusing to talk anymore about my decision. I could not understand why Mom was so upset and rejected me for joining a church. Could Mom not be happy for me once in my lifetime? Seriously, she could not approve of my going to church. Could she not hear how happy I was? I had experienced true peace, love, and forgiveness that I wanted her to experience.

I grieved for my mother because she was so hardened towards God. For months I grieved because she was rejecting Jesus Christ. I knew He was her answer to forgiveness and purpose in her life. Mom had lived all her life in the kingdom of darkness, and I wanted her to live in the kingdom of light. I wanted her to accept Christ so she could also go to heaven when she died. I worried constantly about my mother. One day while driving down the road, I heard these words in my spirit:

"You do not have to die for her; I already have."

I realized I had to give Mom to God and let *Him* change her. I chose to accept His peace that passes all understanding and live *my* life full of hope. *Mom was not too hard for God.*

From the author Sheila Walsh's book, *Loved Back to Life*, she writes:

"Every once in a while, a ewe will give birth to a lamb and reject it. There are many reasons she may do this. If the lamb is returned to the ewe, the mother may even kick the poor animal away. Once a ewe rejects one of her lambs, she will never change her mind. These little lambs will hang their heads so low that it looks like something is wrong with their necks. Their spirit is broken.

These lambs are called "bummer lambs." Unless the shepherd intervenes, that lamb will die, rejected and alone. So, do you know what the shepherd does? He takes the rejected little one into his home, hand-feeds it, and keeps it warm by the fire

He will wrap it up with blankets and hold it to his chest so the bummer can hear his heartbeat. Once the lamb is strong enough, the shepherd will place it in the field with the rest of the flock. But that sheep never forgets how the shepherd cared for him when his mother rejected him. When the shepherd calls for the flock, guess who runs to him first? That is right, the bummer lamb. He knows his voice intimately. It is not that the bummer lamb is loved more; it just knows intimately the one who loves it. He just believes it because he has experienced that love one on one."

I could not have said it any better than what Sheila Walsh wrote in her book. I was the "bummer lamb" rejected and broken, kicked away by my parents. If I kept my ear listening for Jesus' voice, I felt loved, accepted, and forgiven. I determined that I would only hear what God said about me and not listen to the voice of shame and rejection.

That same year I had to have an abdominal hysterectomy due to the difficulties I had during my pregnancy with Laurie and Angela. I came home from the hospital, grieving the loss of my ability to have any more children. I especially wanted to have a son for Chris. I woke up one morning and started reflecting on what a miracle it was that we had two daughters. I realized I needed to be thankful for our daughters and praise God for His goodness and mercy. It was my praising God for what we did have that delivered me out of my deep depression and grief.

I had such a hunger for a deeper understanding of Christ. I began attending another church closer to our home. I placed Chris' name on the church's prayer chain and left tracts all over the house. I placed a prayer cloth that I received in the mail under Chris' pillow. He was furious with my bold attempts to convert him. Larry Bennett, the friend that Chris told at Twin Oaks Restaurant that he was going to marry me, had gotten saved and was attending the same church. I had invited Larry and Pastor Chapman to come to our home to talk to Chris about salvation. The day they were planning to visit, I called Pastor Chapman, trying to cancel the appointment. I was scared that Chris would be irate, and I had to live with him after their visit. I nervously said, "Pastor Chapman, maybe we should not try to push him; after all, Chris is very stubborn. I will have to live with the consequences after you leave."

Pastor Chapman responded, "Where am I going to push him—hell #2? You see, he is already headed to hell by refusing to surrender and accept Jesus Christ as his Savior."

It was the evening of November 7, 1972, when Pastor Chapman and Larry rang the doorbell. It was a tense moment as I peeked from the kitchen to see if Chris would let them in our home. He was not expecting them because I had not told him they were coming. I knew Chris would have left the house if he had known. When Chris saw Larry, he could not turn them away. He invited them into our living room to visit. I nervously served them coffee, and Pastor Chapman got down to business. He started talking to Chris about salvation. Chris was stubborn, and he peppered the pastor with every objection he could. Pastor Chapman never lost his focus as he came back with every scriptural response to counter Chris' punch. In a soft voice, Larry shared how Jesus Christ had changed his life. Chris started to soften just as the phone rang. *Who would be calling us at this hour?* I thought.

I quickly jumped up from the sofa and ran to the kitchen so they could keep talking. I answered the phone. It was the pastor's wife, Sarah, calling to talk to her husband. I whispered, "Could the pastor call you back? He is talking with my husband about being saved."

Her voice cracked as she said, "A loaded freighter, the *African Neptune*, has just slammed into the side of the Sidney Lanier Bridge on Highway 17. The crash downed two spans on the south end of the sixteen-year-old bridge. Four hundred and fifty feet of the mile-long bridge has fallen into the water, and the prow of the freighter is badly damaged. At least five people are confirmed dead, and six more are missing from the cars that plunged from the bridge into the pitch-black water. Helicopters and divers have been called in to help local rescue units. They are calling for pastors to go to the hospital to console family members."

I responded by saying, "Oh no, how horrible. That is heartbreaking. I understand, Sarah; I promise I will tell Pastor Chapman to go to the hospital as soon as he finishes getting my husband converted." I hung up the phone, and as I entered our living room, I saw Pastor Chapman, Larry, and Chris, down

215

on their knees praying the sinner's prayer. Tears were streaming down all their faces, as well as mine.

We all held hands and prayed for the people who were missing, injured, and for those families who had loved ones that died from the tragedy at Sidney Lanier Bridge. Pastor Chapman raced to his car to go to the hospital to join other pastors consoling family members.

In one moment of time, life had changed for so many, including my husband.

— CHAPTER 8 —
PITIFUL OR POWERFUL?

I began working for Pastor Chapman as his personal secretary. I did whatever he needed. He asked me to take over teaching and to counsel the teen girls on Wednesday night for a youth leader who had moved out of state. Chris was operating the bus ministry and was appointed as an elder, although he was a new convert. I began teaching a class for teenagers and meeting with some of the teen girls for counseling. As I listened to their stories of heartache about their hard life, I would feel like jumping over the desk to shake them. They thought that was a hard life. I wanted to tell them what a hard life really was. They had to choose either a *pitiful or powerful life.*

I had chosen to live a powerful life—no more pitiful me. In the stillness of my prayer time that night, I was impressed with the compassion of the Lord for these teen girls. The Holy Spirit laid on my heart how He was listening and that He cared deeply about these girls' lives, even if I did not. He reminded me of the suffering of Jesus Christ at Calvary. I had suffered nothing to compare with what God's Son had endured. Their lives mattered to God, and they better matter to me. I immediately got on my knees and repented of my arrogance. I asked God to change my heart and give me His heart of compassion for the teenagers.

One stormy morning when I arrived at the church, Pastor Chapman heard me walking toward my office. He called out, "Iris, please, come see me as soon as you can."

"Yes, sir," I answered. "I will be right there." I quickly took my wet coat and threw it over my chair and rushed to the pastor's office with a pen and pad in my hand.

After some awkward silence, he immediately got to the point. "Iris, I have received a phone call from one of my founding elders. He is very upset about what you are teaching in your teen's class and your counseling of the teen girls." I responded, "That elder's daughter is in my class and has a great passion for knowing more about the Lord and His Word. I am excited to see her change and influence the other girls to hunger for more of God."

The pastor tried to be kind but firm. "I'm sorry, Iris, but you will no longer be working with the youth."

"Please, Pastor Chapman, what have I done wrong? I love working with the teens, and my class has grown more than any other class."

"You have offended an elder about your focus on the Holy Spirit." I had recently heard a teaching by an evangelist on TBN television about being baptized in the Holy Spirit, which was available to anyone who was saved and wanted to receive.

Jesus was talking to His disciples on the Mount of Olives forty days after His crucifixion. It was just before He ascended back into heaven.

In John 14:26 (ESV), Jesus is telling His disciples that He is going away. He tells them not to worry. He says, "But the Helper, the Holy Spirit, whom the Father will send in My name, He will teach you all things, and bring to your remembrance all that I have said."

In John 16:7 (AMP), Jesus says, "But, I tell you the truth, it is to your advantage that I go away; for if I do not go away, the Helper (Comforter, Advocate, Intercessor, Counselor, Strengthener, Standby) will not come to you; but if I go I will send Him (the Holy Spirit) to you (to be in close fellowship with you)."

The book of Acts was written to the lovers of God. Passion Translation Bible.

The last words that Jesus spoke to His disciples (lovers of God) were:

"Do not leave Jerusalem but wait here until you receive the gift I told you about, the gift the Father has promised. For John truly baptized with water, but you shall be baptized in the Holy Spirit not many days from now. I promise you this—the Holy Spirit will come upon you, and you will be seized with power (Acts 1:4-8, TPT).

"On the day of Pentecost (The Feast of Harvest), Jesus's words were fulfilled" (Acts 2:1 NIV).

I asked God to baptize me in His Holy Spirit. God has demonstrated His grace and His forgiveness every day as He has promised in His Word. My heart was hungry for more of God and a deeper understanding of the Holy Spirit. I desperately wanted to hear the Holy Spirit's voice more clearly and learn more about this spiritual awakening in me. All I knew was that I desired and needed the Holy Spirit's power to live a victorious life from my traumatized past and present struggles.

Our family began attending Christian Renewal Church in Brunswick, Georgia, which was meeting on Sundays at Howard Coffin Park Recreation Center. Pastors William (Bill) T. Ligon, the former senior pastor of First Baptist Church, Pastor Calder Kinney of New Hope Methodist Church, and Jim Adkins, also of First Baptist, founded the new non-denominational church.

One summer morning, as we were leaving church, Laurie looked at me with disappointment and said, "Mom, it's pouring down rain. How are we going to get to our car?" We had arrived late and had to park in the last row, which was a long walk to the church at the recreation center. Chris was unable to attend with us that Sunday because one of his employees was ill and could not work. He had to go to cover his shift.

As we stood there looking at each other, I smiled and said, "There is no lightning, and it's a warm day, so we are going to dance in the rain to our car!"

Angela looked at me like I had lost my mind and said, "What? You have always made us come into the house when it was raining."

I grabbed each of their hands and said, "Not today! Let's go!" I looked over at my girls' giggling, dancing in the rain, and suddenly I had a flashback to my own childhood. I realized I had never had a moment like this with my mother. My tears mixed with the rain and ran down my face. My heart filled with joy and thanksgiving in gratitude to God because my daughters did not know the pain that I had known as a child.

Christian Renewal Church moved in 1978 to a new location at 4265 Norwich Street, Brunswick, Georgia, where they continued to carry out their local and world vision. They had built Christian Renewal Church upon "Imparting the High Priestly Blessing," as God had given Moses.

The High Priestly Blessing: "And the Lord spoke to Moses, saying; 'Speak to Aaron and his sons, saying, this is the way you shall bless the children of Israel. Say to them: The Lord bless you and keep you; The Lord make his face shine upon you and be gracious to you; The Lord lift up His countenance upon you and give you peace.'"

Numbers 6:22-26 (NKJV)

Pastor Ligon began speaking *The High Priestly Blessing* over our congregation each Sunday. He is a humble, gifted pastor. I knew he spent time with Jesus when I heard his preaching of God's Word. He had such love and compassion for his congregation.

In my personal Bible study time, I then began also studying Matthew 19:17-19 (BSB). I was challenged in my belief with Jesus' response. He was being asked about what is good. Jesus answered, "Why are you asking Me about what is good? There is only One who is good, but if you wish to enter into life, keep the commandments." Then He was asked, "Which ones?" and Jesus said, "You shall not commit murder; you shall not commit adultery; you shall not steal; you shall not bear false witness; *honor your father and mother*, and you shall love your neighbor as yourself." I discovered in my research that the fifth commandment, *honor your father and mother*, has a promise attached to it, namely, "...So you will live well and have a long life." God desires for us to have an abundant long life of loving Him and loving each other.

In my conversation with God, I questioned His Word. "Have you not watched my life with my parents? You could not be asking *me* to honor *my* parents?" I kept trying to push the verses about honoring my parents out of my anxious thoughts. *I even thought of tearing that page out of my Bible.* I agonized about coming to grips with how to forgive and honor my parents after all they had done to my brother and me. I finally felt free from my parent's emotional, physical, and sexual abuse, but I still was captured, chained, in my mind with this bondage to my past. When they did call me with their constant anger, I couldn't just hang up. I was the problem solver, *the fixer*, and I was convinced I could fix them. I always saw every man like I saw my father. Every time the pastor would preach on God being a Father, I saw my father. My father was a man of lies and could not be trusted. A man who did not have unconditional love. A man who, by his choices, deserved to be separated from God for all the pain he caused so many. I believed he in no way deserved to go to heaven.

For several weeks Pastor Ligon continued teaching the congregation on *The High Priestly Blessing*. I began to understand the biblical foundations for *Imparting the Spoken Blessing*. God had commanded Moses and Aaron to bless His people. He took us all through a journey from the Old Testament to the New Testament to see God's blueprint for *Imparting the Blessing*. He taught us how to break any spoken verbal curse over our lives using the redemptive power of *The Blessing*.

God wanted to impart His *forgiveness* and His *Spoken Blessing* through me. I knew I had to surrender and accept God's forgiveness for myself and my parents.

I knew I was not capable of forgiving them. I also knew God was capable.

One day, filled with boldness and a commitment to obey God's Word—even though I did not feel like forgiving my father, I went to visit him. I believed I did not have to feel like it to give forgiveness. If I obeyed His Word, *God's* forgiveness would flow through me. I drove to my father's one-bedroom apartment. I believed God was going before me. I knew it was time for me to release my father and me from the unforgiveness and bitterness in my soul that I had struggled with all my life.

I parked my car and then slowly walked to his apartment. When I knocked on his door, Annette, his tenth wife, who was a very simple-minded, childlike, uneducated woman, answered the door. She smiled and invited me in. As I sat down on my father's well-worn sofa, I looked around at his shabby one-bedroom apartment, which had a strong smell of musty cigarettes and burned holes in the carpet. His stack of newspapers and lottery mail piled higher than his end table next to his recliner. He believed he was going to win the lottery and his life would change, as he wasted his life away watching TV and sleeping in his recliner. I asked Annette if she would allow me to speak to my father in private. She left the room, and I stumbled with my words, but finally, I bravely said, "I have chosen to forgive the emotional, physical, and sexual abuse you have done to me all of my life."

He arrogantly stood up out of his recliner, hitched up his pants over his pot belly, towered over me, and in defiance raised his voice as he angrily responded, "You are a crazy girl. I have never done anything to you."

I was in shock; it took my breath away. I was so surprised, and for a moment, I began to doubt it myself. I looked away and began to tremble, then suddenly the boldness came, and I knew now was his time to face the facts. I stood up with my shoulders back as we locked eyes. I was determined, and I was not going to back down, "I do not care if you acknowledge it or not; I still forgive you. I will no longer carry unforgiveness in my heart toward you. I choose to release you and myself from any unforgiveness. You are who you are. There is nothing I can do to change you. Only God!" My eyes welled up with tears as I said, "Dad, if you want the peace that I now have, you should accept Jesus Christ into your heart and ask for His forgiveness."

He slumped into his recliner defeated, and with his head lowered, he whispered, "It was the alcohol; you cannot blame me for what I did when I was drinking."

I sat down on the footstool in front of his chair and said, "Dad, look at me." I grabbed his chin and turned him to face me and said it again, "Look at me! I accepted Jesus Christ, and because of what Jesus Christ has done in my heart, I can forgive you even if you do not accept my forgiveness." He looked down with despair, and I asked, "If you died tonight do you know where you would spend eternity?"

He bowed his head and mumbled, "No."

I replied, "Would you like to accept Jesus Christ by repeating after me the prayer of salvation? Then you will know that you will go to heaven." He looked up and shook his head, yes. I boldly said, "Repeat after me: Dear Lord Jesus."

Dad repeated, "Dear Lord Jesus." I slowly continued, "I know that I am a sinner, and I ask for Your forgiveness. I believe You died for my sins and rose from the dead. I choose to turn from my sins and invite You to come into my heart and life. I want to trust and follow You as my Lord and Savior."

He slowly repeated every word. I then said, "You should go to the altar at Christian Renewal Church on Sunday and tell someone. You can also go to the altar for additional prayer." I wanted to cover all my bases in case I had not done everything right to lead him to salvation. For a moment, I felt compassion for this broken-down man whom Satan and his kingdom of darkness had mastered all his life.

I knew I had just begun a journey of forgiveness and healing from the pain of my memories by bringing light into the darkness.

I smiled as I remembered that angels rejoice when a sinner comes home. Can I be honest? On the day that I released my father by forgiving him, I still did not want my father's mansion in heaven close to mine.

God is the Potter! Let me be the clay!

CHAPTER 9

I AM WHO YOU SAY I AM

Chris and I were very involved in church. Laurie and Angela were helping as leaders in the youth group. Every time the door opened, we were all excited to be at Christian Renewal Church. We all loved our Pastors, William (Bill) Ligon and Calder Kinney. Another dear friend who I respected and loved was Billy Godwin, whose ministry was based out of Christian Renewal Church. He traveled all over the world in his teaching ministry. He often phoned me when he returned from wherever he had been preaching. He was such a mentor to encourage and correct me. He founded a Christian training school in Germany, which sent out missionaries. He often reminded me, "Iris, there is a tragedy worse than death; it is not that people die, but that their dream dies within them while they are still alive. But not you, Iris, because you are going to fulfill your dream." I loved my friendship with Billy. He died not long after speaking those words to me. I miss him and his encouraging talks.

As we were leaving church one Sunday, Pastor Bill Ligon stopped me in the hallway and asked me to schedule an appointment to come see him at his church office at my convenience.

When I arrived for our meeting, Pastor Ligon asked, "Is that your father seated in the back of the church, while I have been teaching the significance of *Imparting the Blessing* on ourselves, spouse, and children from Numbers 6:22-26?"

"Yes, Pastor Ligon, it is."

"Would you consider having your father impart a spoken blessing over you?"

Surprised, I responded, "Pastor Ligon, I do not think he understands what *Imparting a Spoken Blessing* means or even if he would be willing to do it."

He said, "Tell him not to worry. I will write the words for him to speak over you."

I timidly said, "I will talk to him, but I'm doubtful he will do it."

Pastor Ligon smiled, saying, "Don't you worry. Let's pray and leave it in God's hands to handle your father."

I went back to my father's apartment and cautiously asked him, "Would you be willing to be part of a ceremony where you would speak a blessing over my life? Do not worry; Pastor Ligon will have the words written down for you to speak."

He hesitated and looked confused, but he answered, "Yes, I guess, as long as that is all I'm expected to do." I was shocked that he had said yes without arguing. He did not balk at standing before a congregation to speak a blessing over me.

I was so excited driving home. I ran into our home. I was out of breath as I told Chris about my father agreeing to Pastor Ligon's request. Then I said, "Honey, I think we should ask your dad to join us by speaking a blessing over your life, too."

Chris paused for a moment as he absorbed the idea. "I think that would be great. I will call him and invite him to speak a blessing over me, too." We decided to renew our wedding vows and include our fathers speaking a blessing over us at the end of the ceremony. It was our twentieth wedding anniversary when the day finally arrived for our ceremony. I had coordinated so many other weddings in the church; I was extremely joyful to coordinate my own.

Our church friends brought food and even a wedding cake to serve at our reception. I wore a simple but elegant off-white wedding dress, and Chris was handsome in a blue tuxedo. With our friends and family attending and the music softly playing, Chris and I walked down the aisle to stand before Pastor Ligon, waiting at the altar. We exchanged our wedding vows, dedicating our love to each other once again. At the end of our vows, Pastor Ligon called for both of our fathers to join us at the altar. Pastor gave each of them a handwritten scroll containing the words of a *Proclaimed Blessing*. Chris' father, Rudy, choked back tears as he spoke the *Proclaimed Blessing* over Chris. My father then opened his scroll slowly, speaking a Proclaiming Blessing over me. Then Pastor Ligon asked both fathers to lay their hands on our heads as the pastor concluded the ceremony praying *The High Priestly Blessing*.

It was such a moving and powerful ceremony. There was

not a dry eye in the room. At this time, no one knew the full story of the mental, physical, and sexual abuse in my past I had experienced from my father. I did not want to forgive my father because of the pain of abuse he had inflicted on me and my brother for years. The fact that my father would stand before a congregation and speak a blessing over my life was true evidence that God had converted my father by changing his heart. God's mercy is new every morning. It was because of Pastor Ligon's teaching on forgiveness that I chose to accept the truth of God's promise that He would impart His forgiveness through my act of obedience. I had no idea how that act of forgiving my father would change my future.

My love for coordinating weddings was one of the ways I continued to serve at our church, Christian Renewal. Several times a month, I helped coordinate wedding receptions. I loved directing the weddings, but I was quickly getting burned out. I remember feeling bitter standing in the kitchen at the deep sink washing the piled high, dirty dishes from one of the wedding receptions. Everyone else was leaving the building. Of course, some were asking as they headed for the door, "Can we help you, Iris?"

"No, thanks, go on," I insisted. "Thank you, but I can handle it." Then I grumbled and complained as they walked out together, arm in arm, laughing and talking as they headed to their cars. They left me to finish the dishes and all the cleaning before Sunday's services. I arrogantly said out loud, "I don't need anyone; I can do this all by myself!" Standing at the sink, I heard these words as clearly as if someone was standing next to me, speaking to me:

"You will not ask for help because you do not want to share the glory."

My heart was exposed, and I knew it was true. I did not want to share any of the praise. I wanted everyone to brag about what a great job "I" was doing. I knew that was my very problem. I wanted all the praise for doing the work and refused to ask for help so others would not get any of my accolades. From that day forward, I began pursuing the most talented, gifted, and smartest people to be on any of my committees that I had the privilege to serve. I was no longer intimidated to lead a group of strong leaders who could do it better than me. It freed me from the desire to get all the glory for any work I was doing. I began to get out of the way so God could receive the glory and others would be appreciated.

To be honest, there were still times when I chose to listen again to the enemy of my soul. I was ashamed that while God was showing me tremendous favor, revealing His love and His power, that I would allow myself to turn back to my carnal nature. I chose to forget that *I had the power from God's Word and His spoken blessing over my life* to overcome the curse of the words my parents had spoken over me from my past. Those negative, destructive thoughts were like heavy chains attached to my past behaviors and beliefs about myself. I believed that I would never be free from those thoughts like I believed I would never be free from my earthly father. So, therefore, what I believed I received! Negative thoughts about myself controlled me. I had a new heart, but I still had my old mind. Shame and guilt still harassed me, especially after God would do something mighty in my life. The old patterns of belief about myself would return like a broken record, telling me I was a failure, I would never amount to anything, I was not worthy of love. Satan is the father of lies.

Pastor Bill Ligon would preach on forgetting the past and press on toward the high calling in Christ Jesus. I listened, but...

There lies the confusion; I was told to forget the past

but the past would not forget me.

One afternoon I had a revelation about God's Word for me. I knew and believed that God has a great love for us because He sent His Son, Jesus, to take our punishment upon Himself; Jesus' death did not only take my sins, He restored my broken relationship with God. I seem to always live under the *shadow of shame.*

I felt shame for feeling shame.

Jesus, the founder and perfecter of our faith, who for the joy that was set before Him endured the cross, *despising the shame,* and is seated at the right hand of the throne of God (Hebrew 12:2, NKJV). Jesus felt the *shame* and took *my shame* upon Himself. Of course, He took my sins, but thank God He also took my guilt and shame. Before the fall of Adam and Eve, there was no *shame* (Genesis 3:7-10). Therefore, now that Christ has died for my sins, there is no shame. I had to choose to change my thoughts about any *guilt* and *shame* that I struggled with day by day. I chose to *despise the shame* and give it no place in me.

I began journaling my honest thoughts and feelings about any *unforgiveness, fear, insecurity, guilt,* and *shame* that were tormenting me. I wrote every ugly thought and feeling I was having. I would find a scripture in God's Word that would cover whatever I was going through. During prayer, I would give those words I had journaled back to God. It began to be a life-changing tool; if I stayed consistent and disciplined, I would be able to conquer...a strategy for all.

We were faced with new challenges after the bridge fell; no one could travel across the bridge to Jekyll Island. Traffic was detoured away from Highway 17, where we owned and operated both of our Car Care Centers. Our business came to an abrupt halt without the visitors' traffic traveling down Highway 17. We knew we had to make a move to survive the financial crisis. Chris' mother, Eva Lou Welch, had died of colon cancer in October 1985. We knew it would be difficult to leave Chris' father, Rudy, sister, and brother-in-law, Glinda and Ray Thomas. We also knew there were no jobs available anywhere near Brunswick, Georgia. We visited Jacksonville, Charleston, Atlanta and could not feel any desire to live in those cities.

When you do not know what to do, rest,

God will provide you with a plan if you just wait upon His direction.

Our oldest daughter, Laurie, had finished two years at

233

Brunswick Junior College. She did not want to stay in Brunswick and finish her last two years. Laurie came to us asking to help her move to Greenville, South Carolina, and finish her college at a very disciplined university. During those two years, while Laurie was finishing her college classes, I would visit her in Greenville, South Carolina, or she would drive home to see her daddy. Once Chris went with me to Greenville to visit Laurie and the university she was attending. Greenville was not a city that was on our radar at all. While we were visiting, we both had a strong desire and excitement to sell everything and move to Greenville.

Chris decided to visit the Goodyear Tire and Rubber Company's main store located on Haywood Road in Greenville. It was only a few blocks from our hotel. He wanted to inquire about any opportunities available to work in one of the Goodyear stores. He was gone for a couple of hours when he walked back into the hotel room with a surprise for me. "Honey, let's go home and start packing; we are moving to Greenville, South Carolina! After speaking with the store manager, I was offered a job with Goodyear at the main store on Haywood Road. I accepted the position, and I need to move here because I start working in two weeks." I knew it was the right decision but moving in two weeks! God's plan comes with His provision to do it. Chris moved to Greenville in October of 1990 and stayed in a cheap motel that had unmentionable things going on hourly.

After Laurie had finished her junior year, Chris and Laurie moved into a nice apartment while we made the transition from Brunswick, Georgia. I stayed behind in Brunswick to sell the two businesses and our home. We looked like the *Beverly Hillbillies,* going back and forth from Brunswick to Greenville every weekend carrying a load of furniture in the back of Chris' truck. My friend, Pat Ulmer, was showing any interested buyers our home while I was in Greenville. After selling our home, we moved Angela and her son, Caleb, to Greenville to join Laurie in July of 1991. Laurie graduated that summer of 1991.

God's plan does come with His provision to do it.

— CHAPTER 10 —
I HEAR ANGEL WINGS

It was November 24, 1993, the day before Thanksgiving. We had rain showers throughout the day. I finally went to bed at 11 p.m., exhausted from the day of cleaning and cooking to get ready for tomorrow's Thanksgiving meal with our family. I was awakened during the night with a sense of alarm. Immediately I went into prayer, not knowing who I was troubled in my spirit for.

Suddenly, I saw a vision of my mother in a motel room lying on a bed, dying; and she was reaching out to me saying, "Iris, help me." I began to cry and moan with such grief it woke Chris. Startled, he said, "Honey, what is wrong?"

"I just had a vision of my mother in a motel room dying, crying for my help. I have to find her before it's too late."

Chris tried to calm me down. "I'm telling you, it's just a bad dream."

"I know my mother is dying; I must help her."

"What in the world are you going to do?" Chris asked.

"I do not know, but I cannot do it from bed."

I got out of bed and called Mom's home several times with no response. I knew if Joe, her husband, did not answer the phone, it meant something must be wrong. I immediately called her best friend, Frieda, in Haledon, New Jersey, at 2:15 a.m. and woke her up. "Frieda, when was the last time you talked to Mom?"

"We spoke on the phone yesterday," Frieda whispered, not to wake up her husband, Karl.

"Something is wrong. Mom needs help; she is dying."

"What in the world makes you believe that, Iris?"

"I had a vision where I could see my mother dying in a motel room. She was reaching out to me, calling my name, asking me to save her."

"Oh honey, that's just a bad dream. Your mother is at home fast asleep. I talked to her yesterday; she sounded fine."

"That is what Chris keeps telling me, but I know it is real. Please, please try to find her."

"Do you know it's 2:30 in the morning?"

Insistent, I replied, "I know. I'm sorry. Mom needs help. Please, we have to find her before it is too late."

"I did receive a call a little while ago. I did not recognize the number, but they did not say a word when I answered, so I hung up," Frieda recalled.

"Please call that number back and find out if it is a motel. Then call me back."

"All right, Iris, but let me try calling her home first, and I'll call you back." Frieda hung up. I began pacing back and forth, interceding in prayer for my mother to be found before it was too late.

Chris begged me, "Please come back to bed, honey."

"I cannot; I know something is wrong, and I have to find her. I talked with Frieda, and she is calling me back in a few minutes." The phone started ringing, and I just stood frozen in the living room, staring at the phone. Afraid of what I was about to hear.

Chris shouted, "Honey, answer the phone."

I walked over and picked up the phone. Frieda said, "I called your mom's home, and Joe finally answered. He had just put his hearing aids back in when I called. I am sure that is why he did not hear your phone call earlier. He did not realize Ida was gone nor where she might be. I called the last call that I received on my phone, and it is a motel. How did you know?"

"Frieda, please call the New Jersey Police. Mom is at that motel, and she is dying." I started crying again. "Trust me, just have the police go to the motel before it's too late." I hung up.

I continued in prayer as I waited. About forty-five minutes later, the phone rang again. Frieda was upset, and her speech was difficult to understand. She spoke in a quavering voice, "I notified the New Jersey Police, and they were able to identify your mother's car in the parking lot of that motel. Ida had registered under a different name. They found her in a room, barely breathing. The ambulance just left with her, headed to the hospital. She is in critical condition, Iris, but she is alive."

"I am on my way. I will take the next flight out. I will call you with the details. Can you pick me up at the airport and take me to the hospital?"

Frieda answered, "Of course, Iris, just let me know where and when, and I will be there."

"Please call me with any updates on Mom's condition."

Frieda was still sobbing; I could barely understand her. She finally calmed down enough to say, "Ida is my best friend. We could have lost her if you had not called. I believe Ida must have been the one who called me from the motel, but she was too weak to speak. Iris, I just do not understand; how did you know what was happening to your mother?"

"Frieda, this was not me. This is because God loves her. God has shown His heart toward Mom. Praise the Lord!" I hung up the phone and turned towards Chris. He looked at me with amazement.

"Honey, they found your mother in a motel, dying? This is unbelievable. I heard what you said to Frieda. God truly is showing His love for Ida."

We bowed our heads with thankfulness, and I prayed, "Thank You, Lord, for saving my mother. I knew You were showing me her dying and burdened me to not quit until I found her. God, You are awesome!" I turned toward Chris. "I need to be on the next flight to be with my mother. She is in critical condition. Frieda will take me from the airport to the hospital when I arrive."

Chris replied, "Of course, honey, you must go, do not worry; we will be fine. Laurie and Angela can handle everything here."

I called the airline and explained that my mother was in critical condition. They were helpful in getting me on the next flight from Greenville, South Carolina (Greenville-Spartanburg International Airport) to Newark Airport, New Jersey (EWR), which had to be a miracle because it was a holiday. I knew that God was preparing my way. I left home at 8 on Thanksgiving morning after I gave Laurie and Angela all the final instructions to finish cooking for all of them. This is not what I had planned for Thanksgiving. Frieda met me at Newark airport when I arrived and drove me to Saint Joseph Hospital. As I began to get out of her car at the hospital, Frieda, knowing that only one of us could see Mom in the ICU unit, said, "I will be back later. Please call me if anything changes with Ida."

The nurse in the ICU led me quietly into Mom's room then left us alone. I sat watching her sleep in a very small room across from the nurse's station. I was gazing out the window, watching the snow beginning to fall. A calm came over me. Mom finally awoke, and when she saw me, she quickly turned her head away in shame and began to cry, softly whispering, "I'm sorry, Iris, you should not have come. I have ruined your Thanksgiving with your family."

"Mom, not as bad as you would have if your plan had succeeded. If you are so desperate to die, then let's do it. You are alive, but you are not living." I slapped my hands together and loudly said, "Let's just end your life today! I have come to be with you so you can die, which is what you want, right?"

"Iris, what are you saying? I don't really want to die; I just do not want to live like this anymore. You do not understand my life. You cannot understand."

I abruptly interrupted her, "This is your fourth attempt to end your life. Let's plan your death right now. Mom, I am here to help you end your life."

Mom responded, "Do not be ridiculous. We would never be able to do it in a hospital and get away with it. The nurse could walk in any minute, and besides, they would just bring me back to life again."

I was walking around the room, looking for something to end her life. "Oh yes, we can. Since you hate your life so much that you are ready to end it, let's do what you want and make sure you die this time."

"You are nuts, Iris!" I was not worried about someone walking in. I trusted God to take care of the details while I took care of His plan. I was wandering around the room, and finally, I found what I was looking for, a Gideon Bible, lying in the nightstand drawer. I opened it up to John 3:16.

"What I am saying is you need to end your life right now and give your life to God. Jesus Christ will give you a *new* life, a life that will be filled with love, forgiveness, and purpose. Is that not what you really want? Is it not time for you to end your way of life and give it all to God?"

Mom bowed her head. "Do you really think God would accept me—after all that I have done? Would I go to heaven?" God's goodness is all over your past. Now that you see it, you don't have to worry about tomorrow...or today, for that matter. "He's the same yesterday, today and forever" (Hebrews 13:8, NIV).

No one will stay out of heaven by being bad; no more than anyone will get to heaven by being good. You will only go to heaven by receiving Jesus Christ.

"Mom, you can believe that you will go to heaven when you die if you choose to receive Christ in your heart and accept what He has already done on Calvary." I opened the Bible and read John 3:16 (KJV), "'For God so loved the world that He gave his only begotten Son, that whosoever believeth in Him should not perish, but have everlasting life.' That says God gave his Son because He loves you, Mom. I am ready; are you ready? You are going to die to your life by giving your life to Jesus Christ to take control and do whatever He wants to do. Please repeat after me, Mom, but only if you mean it with all of your heart."

She bowed her head and repeated my words after me, "Dear Lord Jesus, I know that I am a sinner, and I ask for Your forgiveness. I believe You died for my sins and rose from the dead. I turn from my sins and invite You to come into my heart and life.

I want to trust and follow You as my Lord and Savior. Please help me to have a heart for You and Your ways." It had been almost forty-seven years since Mom rejected my attempt to convert her after I accepted Christ. Only God!

I think I hear angels clapping and a roar in heaven, shouting:

glory to God; a sinner has come home!

CHAPTER 11

ALL BETS OFF

Three days later, Frieda drove Mom and me home from the hospital. Joe had been in very poor health for years. Mom had stopped running her prostitution ring with the mafia a few years earlier because of her health but promised them she would continue to facilitate the gambling, setting odds, accepting, and placing bets, and paying out winnings. I knew I had to have a difficult talk with Mom concerning her new walk in the kingdom of God and teach her why she had to turn away from the kingdom of darkness. I began talking with Mom about her job working for the mafia. She reminded me, "You do understand that I cannot just walk away from the mafia; it could lead to my death."

With a twinkle in my eye and a smile on my face, I confidently said, "Nothing for you to be afraid of anymore. You have already died, and God is in control."

Before I returned home, I arranged for a nurse to visit their home to take care of Joe while Mom recovered her full strength. I took a return flight from Newark Airport, New Jersey (EWR), back to Greenville, South Carolina (Greenville-Spartanburg

International Airport). I received a call three weeks later that Joe had passed away. Mom insisted that she did not want me to make a return trip after visiting earlier in the month. I called my brother, Mark, and he went to be with her during the funeral.

One morning I woke up with a conviction that I needed to take care of my mother since Joe had died. I felt I needed to bring her to Greenville, South Carolina. In my Bible study early the next morning, my Bible opened to the verses, "Take care of any widow who has no one else to care for her. But if she has children or grandchildren, their first responsibility is to show godliness at home and repay their parents by taking care of them. This is something that pleases God" (1 Timothy 5:3-4, NLT). I struggled with God's direction because of our past relationship. It was good that Mom was talking to me on the phone in a civil manner. She had even started attending a Catholic church near her home. I argued with God that Chris would never allow Mom to live in Greenville, so close to us. He would remember how she had treated me over the years. We had two daughters, Laurie, Angela, and our grandson, Caleb, living with us, who would be affected by her moving to Greenville. I prayed, "God, if this is what I am supposed to do, You will need to change Chris' heart so he will be agreeable for Mom to move here."

One evening during dinner, I got up the courage. "You know, honey, I do feel sad to know that my mother is living alone now that Joe has died. All her friends have either died or are no longer in her life. She must be terribly lonely."

Without looking up from his food, Chris didn't even think about it; he just blurted out, "I've felt for some time that we needed to bring your mother to Greenville. I've been waiting for you to want to bring her here." Without any hesitation, he was willing to bring Mom to live near us. This was another reason I loved Chris and why I had learned to *celebrate* him, not just *tolerate* him like I had done so many times in the past. His kind heart was something to celebrate.

It did not take long to finalize our plans. Mom was eager to leave and move to Greenville. Chris rented a truck to drive to Mom's home. I bought a round-trip ticket to fly to get her. I flew to New Jersey, and she used my ticket to fly back to Greenville. Of course, those were the days you could let someone else use your ticket to fly. Not the case anymore. Chris and I packed the moving truck. Some items she had shipped. He drove the truck, I drove her car, while Mom flew to Greenville.

Celebrate, not tolerate!

CHAPTER 12

I GOT THIS!

We moved Mom into her apartment near our home in the fall of 1994. She loved decorating her first-floor apartment and the small garden patio. She proudly hung her New Jersey license plate on the brick wall behind her many plants on the patio. Mom had a gigantic portrait hanging over her bed in New Jersey. An artist in Germany had painted her nude body when she was twenty years old. She was lounging on a sofa with a very small handmade doll in her hand, but her face was replaced with someone else's face. When Oma saw it, she immediately recognized the doll. She knew it was really Mom, her daughter. I asked Mom, "Are you bringing *that* picture hanging over your bed with you to Greenville?" She left the room without answering me. Not wanting to make her angry, I never brought it up again. I was sure it meant she probably was shipping it.

Mom insisted that I visit her every night on the way home from work. One night as I walked into her apartment, she excitedly said, "Iris, come and see how good the picture looks over my bed." My heart dropped, knowing she had shipped *that* picture. I reluctantly approached her bedroom door. She was standing at the end of her bed with a big smile on her face. I looked up at her wall, and to my surprise, she had a framed picture of Raphael's *Cherub Angels*. We both bent over, laughing as she said, "Gotcha!"

Laurie and Angela were getting to know their Oma. They were building memories. I had warned Mom that if she did start drinking again, she would be out of our lives for good. Laurie and Angela undertook the mission to help their Oma change her old ways. It was her habit of cursing every other word. I wanted Mom to stop cursing especially with a five-year-old, Caleb, repeating her every word. I explained to her that cursing was speaking a curse. The girls would make up a word to replace her swore words when she was speaking around Angela's son, Caleb. Every time Mom would try to say a curse word, the girls would loudly interject the word "sugar" to replace the curse word. Mom would laugh, but it did not take long before she started changing her vocabulary; at least, she cut down her cursing considerably.

Mom, after attending our church, Cornerstone, a non-denominational church, chose instead to attend a different church, Christ the King Lutheran Church. Mom liked the church, which was close to her apartment on Pelham Road. Pastor Fox once a month preached his sermon completely in German, her native tongue. She had quit drinking--cold turkey. After over fifty years of alcoholism, she stopped drinking alcohol. Mom would not put anything in her mouth that had alcohol in it, such as mouthwash or any over-the-counter cold medicines.

She knew if she had but just a taste, she would go back to her drinking.

One day after work, as usual, I stopped for a quick visit with Mom, and she announced that she was going to take communion and wanted our family to attend her church to have communion with her the following Sunday. One of the proudest moments in my life was having our daughters at her church to witness us taking Holy Communion at the altar. We approached the altar where the pastor stood to serve us Holy Communion with his golden vessel. I knew that the bread and wine offered for us to partake were representing the body and the blood of the Lord Jesus Christ, but I was concerned about Mom taking the wine that their denomination served. Mom saw in my eyes my concern. She leaned towards me and whispered, "I got this!" As Pastor James Fox approached us, he reached underneath the altar for a different vessel which he only served Mom and me. It was grape juice prepared beforehand because Mom had already decided with the pastor not to partake of the wine. I knew this act of commitment showed how serious she was to never drink again.

Mom's health quickly began to deteriorate, and she was frightened to live alone. We moved her from her apartment into our home. I began to take care of her as much as I could while I still worked. We remodeled the opposite side of our home for Mom to have a bedroom, bath, and living room, which opened to the deck, so she could have her own space. We would also enjoy our privacy.

One morning Chris took Mom with him to the grocery store to do my grocery shopping. When they returned, I reached over and gave Chris a hug and whispered, "Honey, I know Mom is a handful. Taking Mom to the grocery store is a task. I want you to know how much I appreciate you helping me with her today."

He responded, "Ida was no problem. She actually had her grocery items and beat me to the front of the store."

"Are you saying you did not push Mom in a wheelchair around the store?"

Chris laughed. "Of course not. Ida was going up and down the grocery store aisle faster than I could." I did not see the humor. Mom had manipulated me into pushing her everywhere in a wheelchair. She would tell me she was unable to walk very far anymore. She had me giving her baths, styling her hair, dressing her, putting her makeup on, shopping for her while taking her to numerous doctors for check-ups and tests. After Chris told me what Mom could do, things changed as I encouraged Mom to do those things I knew she could do for herself.

Mom began meeting me every evening at my car door as I arrived home from work. I was beginning to dread her living with us, but I also began to see what God was doing in our relationship. Jesus Christ was showing me how to love my mother unconditionally and how to forgive her! Christ showed me how to be patient with her. I looked for opportunities to share my life's testimony of God's grace and forgiveness in me. Mom no longer heard me just talk about the Lord; she saw the change in my heart towards her and my father. She realized that it was God who changed my heart.

She watched the love that Chris and I demonstrated by our tenderness towards each other, how we held hands and were happy when we were together. She admired the man she saw in Chris and realized that she was wrong about how she had felt about him on our wedding day. Chris had always been a good man. He became a great man after accepting Jesus Christ. He was a man of God, who everyone loved, a veteran who always sacrificed for his country and his family. Mom had come to admire him too. She saw how much I trusted and loved Chris. She, too, began trusting him, which was astonishing since she had never trusted a man before. He had a heart after God, and even before he accepted Christ, I believe God gave Chris the nudge to marry me so many years ago. Opposites do attract! He was my perfect soulmate.

One evening as Mom and I sat on our deck drinking our coffee and watching the birds at the bird feeder, Mom asked, "How do you like your job at MCI?"

"Well, Mom, to be honest, I love my job as a supervisor, but I do have a difficult manager."

"What is wrong with your manager?" she asked.

I replied, "She belittles me in front of others. Yesterday she started saying things again that were very hurtful to me. Words from my past that would have devastated me, and I would have believed them, but I now know who I am in Christ." This time I just turned to her in a calm voice and bravely said:

"Your opinion of me does not change my opinion of me.
It only changes my opinion of you."

— Chapter 13 —
I Never Knew You

One December morning, I had only a few minutes to finish my project at MCI Communications. I had to present a report at our weekly supervisors' meeting with my manager. I made a quick phone call to Mom and was about to hang up when Mom finally answered. "What are you doing?" I asked, frustrated.

"Nothing," she whispered.

"Please put the bathroom rugs that are in the washing machine into the dryer for me. I will be stopping at the grocery store after work to get a few things to prepare for the Christmas party tomorrow night. I will be home around six-thirty. Goodbye."

"Okay," she answered. I hung up the phone. I ran down the hall to my manager's office and slipped in before she noticed I was a few minutes late.

After work, it was bitter cold as I hugged my winter coat around me, running across the parking lot to my car. Traffic was terrible, as usual, with drivers not allowing anyone to change lanes. I had to drive around and around to find a parking space at the grocery store. My mind was racing with everything that I needed to do before Christmas. Tomorrow night was the annual progressive Christmas party with Pastor Dale Blair and his wife, Donna, and members of our Bible study group at Cornerstone Church. We had volunteered to host the dessert at our home. The evening would start at Charles and Judy Durham's home with appetizers, then caravan by car to Pastor's Dale and Donna's home for the main course and finish at our home with dessert. Everyone would enjoy each home's Christmas decorations and have a great meal along the way. Then at the end of the evening, we would sing Christmas carols. Tonight, I had to finish baking my desserts so I could finish cleaning the house tomorrow for our party.

I was so excited because this party would give us an opportunity to get to know our new Bible study friends at Cornerstone Church. I loved decorating our home for Christmas. There were stockings hanging on the fireplace mantel, and the nine-foot Christmas tree in the corner was loaded with collectible decorations and hundreds of tiny white lights. Presents were beautifully wrapped under the tree already. I loved buying just the right gift for each person. The sound of Christmas music would be playing throughout our home when the guests arrived. Candles would be lit throughout our home. The front yard was already decorated with a manger, lighted deer, and even colored lights that Chris loved would be wrapped around the shrubs. Chris had worked hard getting the yard decorated early for our party.

This Christmas would be extra special with Mom in our

home, and I was so happy. I still had much to do and more gifts to buy. I rounded the corner of our street with my home in sight. I saw the Christmas lights through the dark. As I got closer, I noticed that Mom was not standing in the driveway waiting for me to arrive. Every day, no matter the weather—even in the bitter cold, she would be pacing back and forth on our driveway, greeting me at my car door before I could get out. How many times had I worked late so I did not have to go home and encounter Mom? I just wanted to be alone with my husband after a hard day at work. The drama began every morning as I would prepare to leave our home for work with her begging me not to leave her, always claiming this was the day she would die. I was exhausted trying to keep her happy.

Tonight, I heaved a great sigh of relief when I saw Chris' car was already home and Mom was nowhere in sight. I would need to hurry to get supper ready. I grabbed the bags of groceries and ran into the side door. I put the groceries on the counter, pulled my coat off in a hurry and threw it over a chair then quickly started across our living room to Mom's bedroom. Chris stopped me in my tracks, saying, "Let her sleep. You can wake her when you have supper ready." I thought to myself, *she never sleeps this time of the day*, but it would be nice to cook supper without her standing over me correcting me on how and what I was cooking. Mom was a fabulous cook, but she had never taught me any of her culinary skills. She complained about our southern meals but refused to cook any longer. I quickly turned and headed back to the kitchen. I felt a heaviness come upon me. I thought, *I must need a good night's sleep tonight, so I will be rested for the party tomorrow night.*

I decided to cook Chris' favorite country-fried cube steak with gravy, mashed potatoes, sweet peas, and biscuits. I began talking to Chris a mile a minute about my day and which desserts I was going to make for tomorrow night. For some reason, I again felt extremely troubled in my spirit and had been that way all day. I kept dismissing that feeling, convinced I probably was anxious about the party being at our home. I didn't even notice that Chris was dozing in his recliner and didn't answer when I asked, "What should I wear for the party?"

Finally, the table was set, and supper was ready when I headed to Mom's bedroom, calling out, "Mom, supper's ready! Let's eat." As I entered her bedroom, the light was off, but the hall light revealed her half-dressed body lying half on and half off her bed. I could hear her struggling to breathe. I called her name again as I turned on her bedroom light. Terror gripped my heart, and my knees got weak. I could not wake her. I started screaming. I saw a letter by her bedside with an empty medicine bottle turned over. Chris heard my screams and ran into the room just as I picked up the letter and read, "I cannot live in pain, and I do not want to be a burden to you any longer. I know I have cancer, and you are not telling me the truth about the tests the doctors have done."

I dropped the letter and screamed, "No, no, no, God please, please do not let her die." Chris grabbed the phone and called 911, then ran to our next-door neighbor, Debbie, who worked in a doctor's office, asking her for help. I kept calling, "Mom, Mom, please wake up!" But she did not move. I quickly turned back to finish reading her letter. She believed she had cancer because her body was in pain and hurting all the time.

I had taken her to several doctors who did tests. Every test revealed no problems except that she had high blood pressure. How could anyone live the hard life she had lived for seventy-three years without it affecting her body in these latter days of her life? I kept crying and pleading with God to save her. "Please do not let her die, not like this." I had already moved Mom back onto the bed when Debbie was by my side, trying to get Mom to respond while she took a wet cloth to her forehead.

Chris went outside to flag the EMS when they arrived. I moved out of the way as the EMS medics came into the room. They started taking Mom's vital signs. There was very little response. They moved her to the ambulance and me to the front seat while one of them continued to work on Mom in the back. Debbie promised to turn off the stove and put up the food, lock up our home and come to the hospital later. I shouted, "Chris, please follow us and meet us at the hospital." He nodded his head, and I could see in his eyes his concern for Mom and me. He followed behind while the sound of the ambulance siren stopped traffic to let us quickly proceed to the hospital. I asked the paramedic, "Is Mom going to make it?"

He answered, "Ma'am, we are doing everything we can."

Dr. Wilson was Mom's primary care doctor and just happened to be working in the emergency room when we arrived by ambulance. They ushered us to the waiting room as they rushed Mom into the emergency room. I couldn't sit down. I just kept pacing the floor, and after about two hours, Dr. Wilson came to speak with us. "We've pumped her stomach. We have done everything we can. Iris, I am so sorry, but your mother is still not responding, and there is very little hope that your mother will live through the night. There is not much else we can do except keep her comfortable." Dr. Wilson walked closer, and she put her arm around me as I began to sob. They had moved Mom to the ICU unit. I sat by her bedside, watching her still body with all the tubes and the sounds of the monitors and machines as they softly ticked, slushed, and beeped, keeping her alive.

I thought about her life and how in control Mom had always been. She had never cared that she was a burden to anyone. This was her fifth attempt to end her life over her seventy-three years of life. Each time, I never believed that she wanted to die. I thought she just wanted attention and to be rescued from the life she was living. So many times, in the past, Mom was kind, loving, and giving, but when she was drinking, which was pretty much all the time, she would change to a very bitter, abusive person with a fiery temper. She was an alcoholic that drank every day and became depressed, critical of others, and would show a raw, violent mood toward me or anyone else in seconds. Mom had changed after my last visit to the hospital in New Jersey. She had quit drinking alcohol after all those years. I had heard numerous doctors say the same thing I was hearing tonight. Somehow, she always survived and returned home. Surely, she would survive again.

I thought about my attitude on the phone earlier in the day. I should not have been so short with Mom. Why did I not see any signs of her wanting to end her life again? I knew I had been staying too busy to put God first in my life. I had neglected my close time of prayer and Bible study every day. I was no longer sensitive to the Holy Spirit like I had been before. The cares of my life were choking out the Word of God. I asked God to forgive me and restore my first love for Him. I had noticed that she had been so calm and seemed happier for the last week. Could it be that she was at peace because she had made her plan and had chosen her time to die? I wish I had known that today was going to be the last time I would talk to Mom. I would not have cared about those stupid bathroom rugs.

Terror gripped my heart. *Will this be the end? Will my mother really die this time? Will she really go to heaven? I cannot imagine that she would spend eternity separated from God* and us. My thoughts were tormenting me with fear about my mother being a murderer, ordering the death of more than one man who had beaten her call girls. I witnessed her tell the hired killer working for the mafia to throw a man's body in the Hudson River. I knew of her cold heart about having so many men killed. How cruel she had been with my brother, Mark, and me, with apparently no remorse about her life and what she had done to us and others. I thought about the adultery she had committed with many different married men, not caring about the families that she had destroyed. Also, the many unspeakable things she did working for the mafia.

I asked out loud, "Jesus, did she really receive forgiveness when she prayed with me at the Saint Joseph Hospital to accept You into her heart?" I knew that I should just believe what the Word of God proclaimed about accepting Jesus Christ. But now that Mom was truly facing death, I was seriously having my doubts about Mom's salvation as the fear of the memories of her life flooded my mind. I knew God's Word is the final authority, and I should not need any other proof. My belief was being tested by the terror tormenting my mind. I prayed and asked God for a sign that Mom would be in heaven. I knew God would answer my prayer somehow, someway.

Chris went home to call Pastor Dale about Mom's condition. Obviously, we will not be able to have the party at our home tomorrow night. I paced around her room, praying, "God, please do not take her until you show me a sign that she will be with You in heaven." It was a long sleepless night, but against all odds, she made it through the night. Chris had called our daughters to come to the hospital. We were all there as Dr. Wilson examined her, but her vital signs were still very weak. She apologized again, "Iris, you need to prepare yourself that she will not make it through another day. There is nothing we can do except to keep her comfortable. Honestly, I do not know how she is still living." Mom had a living will about end-of-life care and medical treatment. There was a dove on her door, signifying do not to attempt resuscitation; just let her go when she died.

Morphine was now her friend. Mom had developed pneumonia from having her stomach pumped because some of the fluid had backed up into her lungs. She remained in a coma, not responding to anyone. I watched her as she lay still on the hospital bed. The roots of her dyed red hair were showing the gray, and the wrinkles on her face told her age. Alone in her room, I yelled out loud, "I never knew you." I was listening to my thoughts racing out of control with fear and bitterness. I was shattered, struggling to cope with her decision to commit suicide again. I was blaming myself for not making her happy while she lived with us; what an impossible task to keep her happy every minute of every day like I had wanted others to keep me happy. I knew only Jesus could give us true happiness. I continued to question my mother out loud as if she could hear me.

"I never knew you! You were never a loving mother! Why? Did you not want to be a mother? Why did you drink your life away? Why were you so indifferent to Mark's and my pain? Did you not want us? Why could you not show us any tenderness?" I agonized. As I stared at her, I wondered, *What hurt you so deeply that you hurt others? I would give my life for my daughters! Why could you not love your own son and daughter? Why did you choose this time of the year to commit suicide? You have always destroyed any happiness that we reached for in our lives.*

Suddenly my heart melted, and I was filled with compassion and love. I stopped rehearsing my own anguish. I cried out to

God, "Help me forgive my mother again for all the things she has done to my family and to me. Help me forgive her for not wanting to live and for choosing to die this Christmas season. Thank You, Lord, for helping me to forgive her actions from her *alcohol addiction* and mental illness that caused so much pain to herself and others."

I knew it was unforgivable to be unforgivable.

Each morning and evening, I was told the same thing. They did not know how she was still alive. I knew God would answer my prayers and show me a sign so I could have peace that she would be with Him. It had been four days. I never left her side but kept praying the same over and over, "Lord, I thank You that You will let me know that Mom will be with You in heaven." As I sat by her bed, I was listening once again to Mom whispering words in German over and over, not opening her eyes. For four days, she had been whispering something in German that I could not understand. I could say *Ich liebe dich* ("I love you"), but I had lost the German language after losing my mother when I was kidnapped by my father. I did not understand what she was saying.

Chris, along with Laurie and Angela, came to the hospital to visit Mom every day. As the girls were with me one afternoon, Mom began whispering the same German words again. She kept repeating them several times while Laurie and Angela were by her bedside. Laurie and Angela simultaneously said, "Mom, what is Oma saying?"

I answered, "I'm sorry, girls, I just do not know. I can no longer interpret German."

Chris took our daughters back to our home to get clean clothes for me to stay another night. While they were gone, suddenly Pastor Fox from Christ the King Lutheran Church, where Mom was going to church, appeared in the hospital room doorway. He was the pastor that held church services in German once a month. Mom loved to attend his services and hear her own native language spoken. I was so excited to see him. I thought, *I have not called you; how did you know that Mom was in the hospital?* He quietly stood in her doorway, looking toward Mom with compassion.

I jumped out of my seat to greet him and said, "Please, come in, Pastor Fox. I am so happy that you have come."

He looked at Mom again and lovingly said, "Ida, Ida, why did you do this? I still have much more work for you to do."

I explained to him, "Mom is still in a coma. She has not responded for four days. Mom has been whispering something in German several times a day. I can no longer interpret German. I do not know what she is saying."

With empathy, he asked, "Do you mind if I pray for your mother?"

"Of course not," I answered. "Please, I would appreciate your prayers for her."

We stood on each side of her bed, bowed our heads, and Pastor Fox began to pray. Then Mom started whispering in

German, as she already had many times. I looked up and said, "Mom is whispering those German words. What is she saying?"

As I watched tears running down Pastor Fox's face, he bowed his head even lower. He slowly translated her words into English for me. "Our Father in heaven, hallowed be thy name. Your kingdom come, Your will be done, on earth as it is in heaven. Give us this day our daily bread, and forgive us our debts, as we also have forgiven our debtors. And lead us not into temptation but deliver us from evil. For thine is the kingdom, the power, and glory forever." Mom was talking to God!

God was talking to me! He had answered my prayer. Praise God. Peace flooded my soul. We both stood quiet as tears poured down our faces. We knew we were in a holy place in the presence of a holy God. I finally got my composure, reached down, touched Mom's face, and gave her a loving kiss on her forehead, saying, "Mom, you can go in peace. I will be all right."

Ida Klara Lina Zubiller went to meet her Lord Jesus Christ a few hours later on December 10, 1996. Her mental anguish, substance abuse, and physical pain were healed as she met face to face the love of a Man, Jesus Christ, the One she had been unknowingly searching for all her seventy-three years of life.

The Potter had finished His chosen vessel.

EPILOGUE

Francois Monet, my biological father, later retired from the French army. He returned to making ballet slippers designed specifically for ballet dancers at the Paris Opera Ballet. He lived a very rich and lavish lifestyle.

Arnold Leroy Arnett Sr. lived with my brother, Mark, and his wife, Olene, for about a year before his death. He had early stages of Alzheimer's disease. They never had a relationship, only an arrangement. He paid Mark monthly for him and his wife, Annette, to live with them. Mark and Olene have also accepted the Lord as their Savior. They still live in Brunswick, Georgia, and we talk frequently.

I never saw Arnold Leroy Arnett Sr. again after I moved to Greenville, South Carolina, in 1990. He had a heart attack and died on March 1, 1997, two months after my mother's death. We attended his funeral, assured that he would meet his God face to face because of his acceptance of Jesus Christ.

Chris' father, Rudy Welch, died from a heart attack in September of 2000.

Our oldest daughter, Laurie, married Derek, and they have two daughters. They live in Augusta, Georgia.

Our youngest daughter, Angela, has two sons, Christopher Caleb Boyd and Timothy Ryan Boyd. Later she married Mark Prince, and they have another son, Micah Tanyon, and a daughter, Bailey Grace. They live in Loris, South Carolina.

Christopher Caleb Boyd has two sons, William Scout and Maxen Basil Boyd. They live in Mauldin, South Carolina. Timothy Ryan Boyd has a son, Layton Rylynn Boyd. They live in Loris, South Carolina.

Uncle Lester and Aunt Emma Bella Harrison have passed away. The Harrison Grocery Store and Coffee Shop where I lived and worked was later rebuilt as a convenience store called Jack Country Mall.

I honor Dad (Fred), Mom (Mary Lou) Gibson, and their younger daughter, Sarah Anne, who have passed away. Their oldest daughter, Freddye Lou Gibson, was killed in a car accident crossing the road to Harrison Grocery Store. Tom Gibson, their son, lives in San Diego, California.

Judy Durham is still coaching, editing, and encouraging writers to complete their books. Judy is now able on Zoom to assist more authors with more opportunities to keep them focused in writing their books.

A FINAL WORD

This book is a testimony of survival, inner healing, forgiveness, and restoration. It demonstrates the power of love and forgiveness through Jesus Christ and His work on Calvary. During our own abuse, failures, and traumas, we often can only remember and feel the pain. It keeps us from knowing the love of the One who loved us first...*Jesus Christ.*

I originally struggled to tell my story in such detail, but I believe those who have experienced mental, physical, or sexual abuse will only relate if I tell the truth, the whole truth, when I share my testimony. I am trusting God with my scars of abuse.

I must tell my story, so God will get the glory!

We all have scars, some visible and some hidden. Christ showed His scars twice to His disciples. Christ never hid His painful abuse at Calvary. He experienced the unfathomable depth of pain and sin for us. His scars also confirm the truth of His resurrection. He conquered death, shame, failure, and unworthiness that attempts to keep us from coming to God. Trust God with your painful memories.

God's goodness is all over your past. Now that you see it, you don't have to worry about tomorrow...or today, for that matter. "Jesus Christ is the same yesterday and today and forever" (Hebrews 13:8, NIV). Just surrender to Jesus Christ. He will open the eyes of your heart to experience all that God has purposed for you. Let Christ heal the mental, physical, and sexual pain from your memories and bring light into the darkness.

Now I can look at my past, no longer the victim, but a survivor—healed, forgiven, and restored because of accepting and having a daily relationship with Jesus Christ in my life.

Arise to your purpose,
Iris Wainright

PROCLAIMED BLESSING

A FATHER SPEAKS A PROCLAIMED BLESSING OVER IRIS

Written by Pastor William (Bill) T. Ligon

Iris may God Almighty, the Father of our Lord Jesus Christ, the One who is longsuffering and slow to anger, abundant in mercy and loving-kindness, grant to you special blessings in your spirit, soul, and body tonight. I come to this moment with fear and trembling because I realize that I have not always been the appropriate father to you. But Jesus changed all that when He forgave my sins and gave me the gift of eternal life. Now I am redeemed through His blood and desire to see you blessed along with your husband, Chris, and your children, Laurie and Angela.

Tonight, I take the Word of God, which is the sword of the Spirit, and I cut you free from the sins of your fathers to the third and fourth generations. I issue this proclamation over your life:

You were named Iris Ruby in a season when your parents did not know God. Although your parents did not know God, God knew you from the beginning and ordained your steps to be a woman of God. Proverbs 31:10 (KJV) says, "Who can find a virtuous woman? For her price is far above rubies." A ruby is a precious stone, deep glowing red in color. The word "ruby" means "excellent spirit." Which spirit you have, Iris. Those who know you clearly see the deep glow of the red blood of Jesus Christ, which covers your head. Through that blood, God made you a covenant woman—a delight to your husband and an inspiration to all who know you.

An iris is a beautiful, stately flower with sword-like leaves and large blooms. Jesus made you to be like a beautiful Iris. "Iris" means "God's promise." You have heard the promises of God and put your trust in them. Therefore, instead of fading, your beauty releases love like the aroma of a budding flower. God has put a sword in your life, which is the Word of God. Your knowledge of God's Word and your loving devotion to it makes you a mighty warrior in the army of the Lord. You hold the sword with your poise and grace and use it with great skill for God's glory.

The peace of the Lord Jesus Christ rests in your household. Your spirit is knit to that of your husband, and your daughters are blessed through you. You open your mouth with wisdom, and the teaching of kindness is in your words. Truly, daughter, the future smiles at you, and the hand of God's blessing is on your head.

—Arnold L. Arnett, Sr.
3-25-1986

After the Proclaimed Blessing, Pastor Ligon asked each of our fathers to lay hands on our heads while Pastor Ligon prayed the High Priestly Blessing over us.

"The Lord bless you and keep you; the Lord make his face *shine upon you and be gracious to you; the Lord lift up His countenance upon you and give you peace.*"

A FATHER SPEAKS
A PROCLAIMED
BLESSING OVER CHRIS

Written by Pastor William (Bill) T. Ligon

Chris, many sons have been born in this world, but you have excelled them all. Your life has encouraged me to put my trust in the Lord. Since you were redeemed to the Lord in 1972, I have watched your life change and found strength and encouragement through you. I chose you for myself when you were only five, and I took you as my son. Now I delight in knowing you as a man as I observe your life devoted to the Lord, your family, and your neighbors. I, too, have been redeemed by the blood of our Lord Jesus Christ and have faith to loose you from the sins of your fathers. Tonight, I take the Word of God, which is the sword of the Spirit, and I cut you free from my sins and the sins of your forefathers to the third and fourth generations of those who have hated God.

This blessing I now proclaim over your life:

You were named Robert Christopher when you were born and found yourself with your mother alone, for your father had left your home. Yet, your name declared your destiny in the hands of Father God, who would never leave you nor forsake you. Robert means "excellent worth," an attribute, which began to surface in your life at an early age. Christopher means "flower of Christ," which you are. Just as your name is a compound of the name Christ Himself, so your life is a multiplication of God's blessings and grace. You are an encouragement to many, a secure foundation for your wife, and an example for your children to follow. The kindness of your hands has encouraged many who know that when your work is done, all is well.

You do not stand in the path of sinners or sit in the seat of scoffers. Your delight is in the law of the Lord, and in that law, you meditate. You are planted by the river of living water, and you bear much good fruit in the kingdom of God. Peace from the Lord is within your gates, and all your endeavors prosper. Your wife is the delight of your heart and your children your crowning glory. Your grandchildren will call you blessed and draw wisdom from your heart. May the peace of the Lord be within your gates, and the arrows of the enemy always fall short at your feet.

—**Rudy Welch**
3-25-1986

After the Proclaimed Blessing, Pastor Ligon asked the fathers to lay hands on each of our heads while Pastor Ligon prayed the High Priestly Blessing over us.

"The Lord bless you and keep you; the Lord make his face shine upon you and be gracious to you; the Lord lift up His countenance upon you and give you peace."

AUTHOR'S PICTURES

1. World War II Ida was her name.

2. Arnold & Ida Wedding It's legal

3. Sgt Arnett baby Iris What Now

4. From Korea Soldier sent 56 ft
letter to war bride

5. Iris's Birthplace above cafe Karlsruhe Germany

6. Ida working for Mafia.
Call & I will be there

7. Ida in CA works at Dance Hall.
dancing with devil

8. I smile because you're my brother, Mark

9. Never will I forget Mom & Dad Gibson

10. New look new life with
    Mom Iris & Ida

11. Our Wedding Mom, Iris,
    Chris & Frieda

12. Miracle daughters Angela & Laurie

13. Mom & Joe Cetrano Wed 1971

14. Chris & Iris Survivors

15. Priestly Blessing with Fathers

16. Priestly Blessing by Pastor Bill Ligon

References & Help

Ligon, Sr, William T. *The Father's Blessing & Imparting the Blessing Study Guide* and *Successful Steps to Maturity*. 2021 <www.thefatherblessing.com>.

Dr. Gothard, Bill. *A Preteen Guide to Conquer Every Trial! "The Inner Mind That Controls Our Life" (Understanding the three levels of your brain)*. 2021 <www.billgothard.com>.

Dr. Leaf, Caroline. *Think, Learn, and Succeed*, 2021 <www.drleaf.com>.

Dr. Hawkins, *David the Trouble with "Trauma Bonding,"* 2021.

Walsh, Sheila. *Loved Back to Life (Bummer Lamb)* sheilawalsh@sheilawalshconnects.

National Suicide Prevention Lifeline: *988* or *1-800-273-8255.*

Samaritans Inc. 24/7 Crisis Services Helpline: *1-877- 870-4673.*

SAMHSA for Mental Illness, Drug, and Substance Abuse: *1-800-622-4357.*

BIBLE SCRIPTURES

Do not be conformed to this world (this age), [fashioned after and adapted to its external, superficial customs], but be transformed (changed) by the (entire) renewal of your mind (by its new ideals and its new attitude), so that you may prove (for yourselves) what is the good and acceptable and perfect will of God, even the thing which is good and acceptable and perfect (in His sight for you).

Romans 12:2 (AMP)

Then the Lord spoke to Moses, saying: "Speak to Aaron and his sons, saying, 'Thus you shall bless the children of Israel. You say to them: 'The Lord bless you and keep you; The Lord makes His face shine upon you and be gracious to you; The Lord lift up His countenance upon you and gives you peace.' So, they shall invoke My name on the sons of Israel, and I then will bless them."

Numbers 6:22-27 (NASB)

Take care of any widow who has no one else to care for her. But if she has children or grandchildren, their first responsibility is to show godliness at home and repay their parents by taking care of them. This is something that pleases God. Now a true widow, a woman who is truly alone in this world, has placed her hope in God. She prays night and day, asking God for his help. But the widow who lives only for pleasure is spiritually dead even while she lives. Give these instructions to the church so that no one will be open to criticism. But those who won't care for their relatives, especially those in their own household, have denied the true faith. Such people are worse than unbelievers.

1 Timothy 5:3-8 (NLT)

...And all the churches shall know that I am he that searcheth the reins and hearts: and I will give unto each one of you according to your works.

Revelation 2:23 (KJV)

Honor your father and mother; and You shall love your neighbor as yourself.

Matthew 19:19 (NASB)

Honor your father and mother, that you may live a long life in the land the Lord your God is giving to you.

Exodus 20:12 (NIV)

If anyone fails to provide for his own, and especially for those of his own family, he has denied the faith (by disregarding its precepts) and is worse than an unbeliever (Who fulfills his obligation in these matters).

1 Timothy 5:8 (AMP)

Bear with each other and forgive one another if any of you has a grievance against someone. Forgive as the Lord forgave you.

Colossians 3:13 (NIV)

For if you forgive other people when they sin against you, your heavenly Father will also forgive you. But if you do not forgive others their sins, your Father will not forgive your sins.

Matthew 6:14-15 (NIV)

Then Peter came and said to Him, "Lord, how often shall my brother sin against me and I forgive him? Up to seven times?" Jesus said to him, "I do not say to you, up to seven times, but up to seventy times seven."

Matthew 18:21-22 (NASB)

But when you are praying, first forgive anyone you are holding a grudge against, so that your Father in heaven will forgive your sins, too.

Mark 11:25 (NLT)

Let all bitterness and wrath and anger and clamor and slander be put away from you, along with all malice. Be kind to one another, tenderhearted, forgiving one another, as God in Christ forgave you.

Ephesians 4:31-32 (ESV)

That You may grant him (power to calm himself and find) peace in the days of adversity, Until the pit is dug for the wicked and ungodly.

Psalm 94:13 (AMP)

When my anxious inner thoughts become overwhelming, your comfort encourages me.

Psalm 94:19 (ISV)

For You formed my inward parts; You covered me in my mother's womb. I will praise You, for I am fearfully and wonderfully made; Marvelous are Your works, and that my soul knows very well.

Psalm 139:13-14 (NKJV)

To appoint unto them that mourn in Zion, to give unto them beauty for ashes, the oil of joy for mourning, the garment of praise for the spirit of heaviness; that they might be called trees of righteousness, the planting of the Lord, that he might be glorified.

Isaiah 61:3 (KJV)

About the Author

Iris surrendered her life to Jesus Christ in 1970. She has hosted a sixty-minute television program, Covenant Woman, that aired on a Christian cable network in Brunswick, Georgia. Through the auspices of Cornerstone Church, Iris and her husband, Chris, directed and hosted couples at marriage enrichment retreats for the building and strengthening of marriages. She has been a youth leader. Iris was a school board chairman for Sonrise Christian School. She has been a speaker at conferences, retreats, and various churches. She is a member of the Author's Guild. Iris is passionate about people accepting Christ and experiencing His abundant life, healing from the pain of their memories from mental, physical, or sexual abuse. Iris lives with her husband, Chris, in Easley, South Carolina. They have two married daughters, six grandchildren, and three great-grandchildren.

To email Iris your testimony,
request Iris as a speaker at your event,
or to purchase additional copies of
I Never Knew You: From Tragedy to Triumph
please contact her at:
AriseToYourPurpose@gmail.com or
website www.AriseToYourPurpose.com